TEACH LF

WR

CRIME & SUSPENSE FICTION
and getting published

Lesley Grant-Adamson

Hodder & Stoughton
A MEMBER OF THE HODDER HEADLINE GROUP

Long-renowned as the authoritative source for self-guided learning – with more than 30 million copies sold worldwide – the *Teach Yourself* series includes over 200 titles in the fields of languages, crafts, hobbies, sports, and other leisure activities.

Library of Congress Catalog Card Number: 95-71307

First published in UK 1996 by Hodder Headline Plc, 338 Euston Road, London NW1 3BH

A catalogue record for this title is available from the British Library.

First published in US 1996 by NTC Publishing Group, 4255 West Touchy Avenue, Lincolnwood (Chicago), Illinois 60646 – 1975 U.S.A.

Typeset by Transet Limited, Coventry, England.
Printed in England by Cox & Wyman Limited, Reading, Berkshire.

Impression number   10 9 8 7 6 5   4 3 2 1
Year   1999 1998 1997 1996

CONTENTS

ABOUT THE AUTHOR

Lesley Grant-Adamson was a well-known journalist when she left *The Guardian* in 1981 to write fiction. Her first novel, *Patterns in the Dust*, established her reputation worldwide as a writer of detective fiction. Her second, *The Face of Death*, made her name as a writer of suspense. Both were published in 1985 by Faber and Faber in Britain and Scribner in the US. She has now written 12 highly acclaimed novels which reviewers have compared with the best of Patricia Highsmith, Simenon, Elmore Leonard, Ruth Rendell and Daphne du Maurier.

Critics have called her 'one of the classiest thriller writers around' (*Sunday Times*) and 'the British writer who has set new standards in crime writing' (London *Evening Standard*). *Cosmopolitan* congratulated her on 'turning the genre into an art form', and P. D. James praised her for knowing 'how to create an atmosphere of unease and incipient horror'. *The Times Literary Supplement* commented that 'her pace never flags. Her novels are constantly diverting'; while the *Daily Telegraph* has found in her work 'shades of John Buchan, even a touch of Dornford Yates. Her stories rattle along.' She is now published by Hodder and Stoughton and by St Martins Press in the US.

This book is based on the course she evolved while teaching students of all ages and abilities in a variety of settings: writers' circles, prisons, the Arvon Foundation and Ty Newydd, and Nottingham Trent University. She was the first crime writer to be appointed a writer in residence at a British university.

She is married and lives in London with her husband, Andrew Grant-Adamson. Together they wrote *A Season in Spain* (published by Pavilion) a portrait of the Alpujarra region of Andalucia and an account of the years they lived there.

INTRODUCTION

We are all born with a talent for storytelling. No one teaches us how to make up imaginative stories when we are small children or how to tell an anecdote once we are adults, we simply know. From time to time most of us spot a story we feel would make a good book, or else we notice someone we think could be an interesting character in a book. Few people, though, have an instinctive understanding of how to develop their ideas into novels. This book can guide you, not by pretending there's an exact formula or by insisting that a 'correct' sequence of events must be followed if a novel is to emerge at the end of all your effort.

Instead, and perhaps unusually, it concentrates on encouraging you to explore your own ideas. From the beginning you will be working on your novel and very soon writing parts of it. That doesn't mean you have to have a clear idea of the story or the characters before you begin, or even much of an idea. The point is to help you work with what you *have* got, not to start from an ideal starting place but from where you actually are. All you need to provide is your enthusiasm and an interest in tackling a crime or suspense novel.

You probably think that to write suspense or crime fiction, and in particular the detective story, an author needs to prepare an extremely detailed outline. Most people believe this. Luckily it's wrong. It would be awful if the intensely satisfying business of imaginative writing were to be reduced to the equivalent of following a knitting pattern. Besides, I have yet to meet a writer in the genre who writes that way, and there are probably as many approaches as there are authors.

Writing is the most personal of the arts. My aim in this book isn't to teach you to use my working methods but to help you discover what best suits you. Neither will I coerce you into trying to write imitations of my novels. What we both want is for you to find your own, distinctive voice as a writer and to complete a novel that is the achievement of your imagination and yours alone.

By all means read the book straight through, if you feel you need to understand the general picture before you begin to work a chapter at a time. That's allowed, too.

1

TO BEGIN AT THE BEGINNING

There are three rules for writing the novel. Unfortunately, nobody knows what they are.   Somerset Maugham

Before every attempt on a novel there are questions to be asked. Let's begin with this one. Why do you enjoy reading crime and suspense fiction?

The predictable answers are that the books tell intriguing stories, they are exciting and they are easy to read. While other novels might provide you with some or all of those things, this genre guarantees them.

And what, exactly, is this genre? No neat answer, I'm afraid, although I offer a detailed one later. For now, let's agree that a crime novel is a novel with a crime at the core of it, whether it's a detective story or another kind; and that a suspense novel is a tantalising tale that might involve a crime but doesn't necessarily do so.

If your honest answer is that you don't read the genre or don't admire it, then it's fair to warn you that you will find it very hard to write. Unfortunately, people are tempted to believe that because a book is easy to read it must have been easy to write. Would that it were true! Don't then, be misled into imagining that a detective story is a simple matter because there are rules to follow; or that a suspense novel is easier yet, because there aren't. In reality, the writer of crime or suspense fiction achieves everything that an ordinary novelist does – but also has to ensure that the result is intriguing, exciting and easy to read.

Reading good authors

The best way of learning about any kind of writing is to read good examples of it. You may sign up for writing courses or read books like this one, on the craft of writing, but they are optional. Reading the work of successful authors, though, is indispensable. This is why, at the end of each chapter, you will find reading lists which will point you in the direction of books worth your attention.

But you know how it is with exciting books: you just have to keep turning the pages. To reap the maximum benefit from your reading, allow yourself to gallop through the story but then go back to the beginning and consider the writing carefully on a slower second reading. Notice, for instance, how individual writers link scenes, introduce characters, change mood, heighten your interest and fight any inclination you might have to put the book down. When you aren't caught up in the dash to the finishing line, you will be able to appreciate their techniques and learn from them.

And as you cut from one respected author to another, you will become aware of their comparative strengths and weaknesses. All authors have their failings as well as their strong points. In a perfect world a tough editor would demand revisions and rewrites until the perfect book emerged. We don't live like that, partly because time comes into it: there's an assumption in genre fiction that writers will produce a steady flow of books.

Notice, then, whether a writer who scores on story and atmosphere might be sloppy about prose, perhaps scattering adverbs and adjectives where one apposite word would provide more effect. Or whether one whose English is elegant, confuses you by an unlikely twist of the plot. Or one who serves up all the rest in splendid fashion, leaves the principal characters too shadowy for your liking. Obviously, your verdicts will be subjective. While you are muttering about situations not being fully explained to your satisfaction, another reader may be enthusing about the subtlety of the novel. But you will be learning what can be achieved within the genre and what perceived failings you wish to avoid in your own work.

Why take to crime?

Have you asked yourself why you want to write this kind of book? Is it that you have a story in mind, and that story centres on a mystery?

Or that you have thought up a character whom you think you could use as a detective? Or you have a professional background, perhaps in the law or police work, that you feel you could draw upon? Those are all sound reasons and not at all uncommon. Any one of them is good enough for a starting point from which to build your novel.

A novel is a way of examining ideas. The author takes a story and uses it to comment on the world in which we live. Through his characters he illuminates human relationships. Every novel is written because the writer is burning to share his ideas with readers. There are no limitations on the ideas he may discuss, the whole gamut of human experience is available. As far as content goes, all that distinguishes crime and suspense fiction is that the novels feature criminality or else characters caught in a tense situation. The genre is ideal for illustrating moral issues. Because we live in a society where the fear of crime is more prevalent than crime itself, novels featuring it are both pertinent and popular.

Criminals make good characters for fiction because they are active, not passive. They are not the stupidest people, either. To commit a crime they have shown initiative and intelligence in the planning, and audacity in carrying it through. Their moral failing is in wanting to do it; their folly is in believing they were merely unlucky to get caught; and their arrogance lies in doing it again. Whether stories centre on criminals or their victims, crime is rich ground for novelists.

Flights of fancy

Being a novelist means viewing life in a slightly different way from the run of humanity. Your friends may be discussing an incident in a down to earth way but your novelist's imagination takes flight. Books begin with questions and one of the most productive is 'What if...?' Asking 'What if?' grants the imagination freedom to wander. It's a question to pose as you plan your novel and one to repeat as the story develops on the page. A novel never arrives in the writer's mind fully fledged but is the sum of the answers to numerous questions.

Suppose you and your friends are leaving a pub when you see a couple having an altercation near a parked car. The man snatches the ignition keys and drives off abandoning the woman. Your friends become very interested in the brief scene but at a more or less factual level. Perhaps they slightly exaggerate what they heard of the exchanges but otherwise they stick to events as they were acted out. They are content to have seen and heard enough to justify a remark about the husband's behaviour being disgraceful or the wife getting her just deserts. The novelist in you, though, is having a wonderful time.

What if, you are wondering, the couple's baby is in its carry-cot on the rear seat? The man didn't seem the type to be tender with babies. Oh, and the woman doesn't have a bag so presumably that's in the car, too. How will she manage without it? But suppose they aren't man and wife. What if he has hijacked the car? As it was exceptionally badly parked, you readily picture it hurtling into the car park, slewing to a stop, doors flying open and the occupants leaping out, the woman trying to run to the safety of the crowed pub but the man cutting her off and grabbing the keys.

A story pieces itself together as fast as kaleidoscope pieces falling into a pattern. It goes like this. A man worms his way into a woman's confidence but while she's giving him a lift he flourishes a knife and forces her to drive him across country. Spotting the pub car park, she swerves into it and tries to escape but he's the one who does the escaping, and in her car.

But wait. That doesn't fit. The woman isn't rushing into the pub begging for a phone call to the police. No, she's walking quietly away from the pub and, now that you come to think of it, she looks guarded. You would expect a victim of a frightening crime to appear shaken. She isn't. Perhaps you have got it the wrong way round. What if she was the one who forced herself on him, and was coercing him into something he couldn't face? What if...?

Is originality crucial?

A story along these lines, reversing the more likely relationship between the two central characters, is more original and therefore more interesting than the first one that came to mind, and it could form the basis of a novel. As I just made it up for you now, I don't think anyone has used it. But I wouldn't be deterred from working it up into a novel, anyway, because once the story and its conclusion were determined, the characters given backgrounds and motivations, and I had settled on a theme of, say, persecution, it would be written in my personal style and would therefore be unlike any other writer's work.

Students have told me they shy from beginning to write because they assume they are called upon to be wholly original, and they fear that, within the bounds of a genre, originality is harder than ever to achieve. Well, anyone who waits for originality will wait a very long time, and it's actually no worse writing within a genre than outside it. Were there to be no star-crossed lovers after Romeo and Juliet?

So when you catch your imagination entertaining you with stories woven around incidents like the one in the cark park, or an unusual person, or a snippet of conversation overheard, or a newspaper story, recognise them for what they are: the glimmers of a novel. As soon as you can, write it all down, the ideas you reject as well as the ones you favour. Additional ones will probably occur to you as you are scribbling. Later on you can sift them, rearrange and rethink, but notions that aren't written down have a habit of being forgotten.

I doubt whether you would want to drag out a notebook in front of your friends, and display your peculiarity quite so openly, but seize the first real opportunity while the ideas remain fresh. It's marvellously entertaining to have the mind of a novelist, but to *become* a novelist imposes disciplines, including note-taking. Otherwise your imaginative flights remain mere day-dreaming.

Meanwhile your friends, who aren't day-dreamers in your league, are moving on to talk about the rotten price of beer, and how much better pubs used to be when you could sit in peace and discuss the rotten price of beer, instead of having to shout against the noise of modernity: piped music, television sets, games machines and karaoke.

Sources of inspiration

People often ask writers: 'Where do you get your ideas from?'. And they can be piqued when you tell them ideas come from everything and anywhere, piqued because that isn't their own experience and they lack any understanding of the novelist's way of looking at the world. Occasionally, though, they too identify a personality or a story they believe should be 'in a book', but as they have no means of using it themselves, they offer it up to any writer of their acquaintance. I don't remember one of these offerings ever being of the slightest use to me, because what sparks off my imagination is different from what sparks theirs or, indeed, yours.

Therefore, I do appreciate that you might well have been wriggling with irritation at my car park example, because that isn't remotely like the story you hope to write and would like my help with. Very well, no more car park scenes. Time to consider what *you* have in mind.

Your starting point

Unless you have already spent a long time toying with an idea, and know what your story is and who the characters in it are, you have probably either thought up only part of a story or else one or two of the principal characters. Perhaps it's vaguer than that: you might just have an urge to use a particular place as the setting, or you might have one scene in your head and not much else. You are in good company, then. P.D. James is one of those who find that their novels are generally born of an urge to use a particular place in a story. Buildings figure prominently in her work; for instance, Sir John Soane's house, transferred across London for *Devices and Desires*. It's also well known that John Fowles's first intimation of *The French Lieutenant's Woman* was an image of a cloaked figure gazing out to sea from the Cobb at Lyme Regis. Such moments are treasure to the novelist. Whatever your starting point, we will start from there.

You will need a notebook small enough to carry around, so that you can record ideas as they occur to you; and either a sheaf of loose sheets of paper that you can clip together or else a big pad from which you can tear pages. A folder, for holding loose pieces of paper, is a boon. A box is better, though, because it can also accommodate your growing manuscript plus any magazines, books or photographs you are using for reference. In addition to the pens you will write with, presumably using black or blue ink, it's good to have a contrasting colour, say red or green, for highlighting specific notes. In Chapter Six I shall discuss equipment again, but at present all you require is the basic means of writing.

Writing it down

Writing a novel is the craft of managing ideas. The fruits of your imagination are more easily considered once they are trapped on paper, so begin by setting down the gist of what you already know about your potential novel. Assuming you have a story, in full or in part, aim to encapsulate it in a paragraph. Since these are merely notes, it needn't be a beautifully written paragraph, merely one that tells the tale in a few lines.

This is how I encapsulated the story that became my second suspense novel, *Threatening Eye*.

Three strand mystery featuring:

1 Man A: porn magazine, prison record, shady behaviour, dog fighting.
2 Man B: hiding out and subject of major manhunt.
3 Colleague who suspects A is murderer. Locate in Hertfordshire.
Black wooden barn could be dog fighting venue.

That was the nub of it. The genesis of the story was a police search for a serial rapist. They had twice questioned a man I knew. I also knew that my acquaintance had a prison record for killing a man and was leading a double life: editor of a respectable magazine plus 'glamour' photographer who preyed on teenage girls. My 'what ifs' exaggerated rape into murder and the rest was sheer invention, except for a welter of topical detail about the resurgence of dog fighting, and topographical and social detail about a typical Hertfordshire village.

Fact and fiction

It is acceptable to take actual people and events as the basis for fiction but they must be distinctly altered. There are both practical and literary reasons for this. You wouldn't want to libel anyone by having him appear, only transparently disguised, as a murderer; and you certainly mustn't use genuine names. Besides, the fewer fetters on your creative powers the better.

Even when you set out thinking you are going to use a real person, you will rapidly drift from him as you dream up ways to enhance the character. There might be more advantage for you as a plotter if the vet changes career and becomes a doctor; the semi-detached where he lives is so humdrum you might prefer him to move into the haunted mansion on the moor; and if he's to endure a skittish wife, the conscientious soul offering her free time behind the desk at the local Citizens Advice Bureau had better be swapped for a flightier model. By the time you have finished playing with him, you will hardly recognise the vet and, more to the point, neither will he.

Conflict and crime

Although they are as varied as the people who write them, novels of every genre and none, are based on conflict. Characters will be in difficulties; through the course of the novel they will struggle to cope; and, by the end, their position will have changed or, at least, their attitude to it will have shifted. In crime fiction the difficulty, or challenge, will be caused by, or result in, a crime. That crime is almost invariably murder because it's the extreme, the one for which there is no possible reparation for the victim and no expiation for the perpetrator.

Common methods of dispatching victims are: shooting, asphyxiating, stabbing, hitting with a blunt instrument, poisoning, drowning, or contriving accidents. To make it convincing, the method should be suited to the character who kills. An habitual criminal might reasonably produce a gun but a housewife is more likely to brandish a heavy pan.

As the genre examines human beings in extreme situations, the story you are developing must allow scope for this. At least one of your characters will be under pressure, and it will increase during the spinning of the yarn. The springboard for your story is most likely to be friction within a family, between friends, neighbours or colleagues. Trouble in human relationships, and the excesses that can result when someone becomes stubborn, jealous, obsessive or vengeful, is a bountiful source of story ideas. Another popular way in which novelists arrive at stories is to imagine how characters might react if their lives were to be disturbed by a repetition, or revelation, of events in the past.

Perhaps you are taking an incident from your family history and using that. When you are working with something from real life, particularly your own family, it's prudent to strip it back to essentials so that you can be clear about the bones of the story. Take the personalities out of it for a moment, because you can be clouded by knowing an enormous amount of detail that would be extraneous to a novel. Reduce Auntie Anna to X and you may realise the shortcomings of her story. With her out of the way, you will be free to invent a more vigorous character to fill her rôle, and to lead the narrative in a direction Auntie Anna didn't go. There's no point in being sentimental. You are seeking a story worth developing into a fiction, not producing biography or a family history.

Keeping it simple

Before you delve into an elaborate piece of work, I should raise a warning flag. You will see from the excerpt I quoted from my notebook that *Threatening Eye* was conceived as a rather ambitious piece of storytelling using three different viewpoints: those of A, B and A's colleague. Perhaps you are tempted to try something similar.

Cutting from one character's viewpoint to another's is, I find, an effective way of heightening tension and speeding the pace of a story. As the reader follows one character through a relatively carefree spell, he can't help but remember what the other character has been up to, and feel apprehensive. Nothing encouraging can be taken for granted. During the good times there will be a current of unease.

But much as I enjoy writing and reading multi-viewpoint novels, it would be a dereliction of duty not to issue a caution to new writers. The more viewpoints you have to cope with, the more complicated the writing. Please think very hard about whether you feel ready to tackle a form that presents extra difficulties. (There's more about viewpoint in Chapter Four.)

I don't urge you to mangle your story so that it re-emerges as a single viewpoint tale. Maybe the most advantageous way to tell it *is* from three or four viewpoints, in which case it could be something to put aside until you are more practised in novel-making. Writer's minds generally teem with ideas and you probably have a more straightforward one jostling for your attention and could proceed with that instead. Having cried 'Watch out!', I leave the decision to you.

The extract from my notebook also reveals that I knew from the very outset that *Threatening Eye* was to be a suspense novel, not a detective story or another kind of crime novel but a suspense novel. It could, you see, have been any of them. I might have concentrated on the police investigation of a series of murders in Hertfordshire villages, in which case it would have become a detective story. A and B would have been suspects until the police proved, despite helpful red herrings from A's colleagues, whodunit. Or it might have been a crime novel centring on A, suspected of murder and finding it impossible to refute without relinquishing the secrets of his own sordid life of crime.

What about your own novel? Do you know yet which broad category it fits? Writing a detective story, complete with sharp-eyed inspector, ever faithful sergeant and none too bright constable, you can be confident that you have pinned on the right label. Otherwise, determining which kind of storytelling best suits your idea might take a little more thought. And having thought, you might later want to revise your decision in the light of new ideas as you explore the story and its characters further.

In its early stages a novel is fluid, nothing is for keeps, and you can reinvent and reject until you settle on something that feels right and goes on feeling right. But as you rethink and revise, don't discard any notes because you might find you prefer an earlier version after all, or at least wish to reconsider it.

The way you tell it

To create a satisfactory novel you need more than a good story and convincing characters. Above all you need to tell the story in the way that allows you to get the most out of it. In the case of this genre, that means whichever way results in it being most intriguing and exciting. Established writers can get it wrong, authors of detective fiction being especially at risk. Because their publishers may demand a new story about Detective Inspector Wizard every year, each idea that occurs to them is tailored to suit the inspector and the chance to write a first-rate novel that doesn't feature him is passed up.

This is why I believe it unwise to commit yourself to a specific kind of crime or suspense novel until you have explored your ideas fully. But should this approach trouble you, and you are desperate to reach for a label right now, then dip into Chapter Three which is devoted entirely to defining the different kinds of crime and suspense fiction.

—— Working on your novel 1 ——

Story

1 Make notes on the story you are planning to use. Don't go into the characters in depth at this stage because you can do so after the following chapter.

2 Indicate the source of information on your notes: newspaper cuttings or television, an anecdote heard or an incident seen. You may need to refer to the source later, to ensure you have made significant changes and disguised real people.

3 Check whether you are yet able to answer these key questions about your novel: who, what, where, when, why and how?

4 Reduce the story to its bones and pinpoint where the conflict lies.

5 Encapsulate the story in a paragraph. Keep it to one page.

Decide whether you feel it has the makings of a suspense novel, a detective novel or a crime novel of a different sort.

Or:

1 Failing a story, write a description, as fully as you like, of one of the central characters.

2 List any tentative ideas for a story. Make a note of what you think is promising about them or why you suspect they won't do.

Or:

1 No character, either? Then write about what you do know so far, perhaps a setting you are keen to use.

Reading list

Paul Benjamin, *New York Trilogy.*
Martin Booth, *A Perfect Gentleman.*
F. Tennyson Jesse, *A Pin to See the Peepshow.*
Mario Vargas Llosa, *Who Killed Palomino Molero.*
Julian Symons, *The Colour of Murder.*
Emma Tennant, *The Last of the Country House Murders.*

2

WITH LUCK AND A FOLLOWING WIND

It's not only a question of the artist looking into himself but also of his looking into others with the experience he has of himself. He writes with sympathy because he feels that the other man is like him.
Georges Simenon

By now you should know rather more about your novel than when you opened this book. Perhaps I have deterred you from attempting something that initially seemed a good idea, or I have convinced you that you are on the right track, but mainly you have benefited from concentrating on the project and encouraging your imagination to explore your ideas. Focusing in this way is the key to making progress. The more serious attention you give the project, the more surely the characters will develop and the story become clearer in your head.

Although you may prefer a quiet place where you can sit with your notebook and writing pad, you can mull over your story while you walk to the shops or catch up on household chores. Do, though, slip a notebook into your pocket because it's maddening to have a brainwave while you are out but no clue what it was once you reach home.

A good story

I keep referring to your 'story', using the word as a blanket term to encompass plot and theme as well, but it also has a narrower sense in novel-making. It may only mean a chronological sequence of events. Ask a friend about the book she's reading and she may reply: 'There's this woman and her boyfriend has left and she goes to the cinema and the reel breaks down and she talks to the man in the next seat and he walks her home and she falls in love with him.' She has reduced it to the meanest level of storytelling. In the hands of a sensitive writer it would be transformed into a poignant tale of heartbreak, courage, disappointment and a quivering trust in the future. In the hands of any old writer there would be colour, characters and adjectives!

An accomplished writer can perform miracles with a weak story, but how do you invent a good one? I believe the essence is to have your characters in an interesting situation, and through the course of the narrative to move them into other interesting situations. Ultimately, a good story is one which engages the reader's attention and keeps it to the end.

A good *crime* story is an eventful one. There's a murder and characters are caught up in its aftermath, which may mean an investigation by police or an amateur sleuth; there are dramatic scenes and an eventual unravelling of the mystery, called a dénouement, during which truths are revealed to the reader and, frequently, also to characters in the tale. A good *suspense* story may be quieter: less activity, perhaps, but a character the reader cares for is under threat.

Stories don't have to be narrated in a straightforward manner because mystery, conflict or tension may be gained by not starting at the beginning of the time sequence. Such decisions aren't necessary until you reach the stage of turning your story into a plot, but you should bear in mind that you will face them. If you suspect your current story is lacking – although you know who does what to whom, and where and when and why and how; and you have a strong character or two at the heart of these events – the likelihood is that it will be transformed when you light upon the best way of relating it.

Timescale

Deciding what span of time is to be covered by your novel may help you resolve some of these issues. Say you were to write a detective story featuring a murder at Bridgwater Carnival. Two equally logical decisions would be either to set it on the night of the carnival, the first Thursday of November, or to expand to take in the whole fortnight of the Somerset winter carnival season. As you see, using real events can prod you towards a solution.

Without a peg of that sort, your answer may be dictated by what your man has to accomplish. If he's to be briefed by his employer, go under-cover at an electronics factory, pursue one lead to California and another to part of the former USSR, investigate the background of the person who hired him, collect secrets from an industrial spy, hand them over to a government agent, have doubts about the government agent and investigate him... A fortnight won't do.

Your central character, also called the hero or protagonist, will have a past but you are unlikely to tell his story from the cradle to the grave, rather to home in on what happens to him at a certain period. Think about how long that period lasts. Eighteen months? Well, it may be that you need to write about the whole eighteen months during which the intrigue builds; but maybe you choose to focus on the three weeks when tensions explode into confrontation. Toy with the options until you know what feels right for your story. The pace you want the novel to have may influence your thinking.

An end in view

Writers argue about how much they need to know about a story before they begin writing. Some of us claim to invent practically everything as we go along, treating the writing as a voyage of discovery. This is something we grow into, as experience teaches us about our individual creative processes and we come to trust our talents and our subconscious to carry us through.

In other words, we take short cuts, not needing to write everything down and refusing to be cast into despair because a character won't come into focus or chunks of the story are vague. What is essential, though, is to understand the purpose of the book and where the chief characters are to finish up. The ending becomes the goal and stays in sight for the duration of the writing.

For example, in my second novel, *The Face of Death*, Peter Dutton pretends an amnesiac woman is his wife and takes her home from hospital. The book is an account of the struggle between them: he dominates her but she tries to escape. Through the course of the story their rôles gradually change: she becomes the stronger character and he cracks. At the end she is renewed, while he is destroyed. All the incidents and minor characters made up during the months of writing were stepping stones on the way to that goal.

Where do you want *your* novel to end up? By deciding whether your hero is to be winner or loser, or how the balance between characters is to be altered, you will be able to proceed with confidence. Writing with a conclusion in mind gives the novel cohesion and prevents your imagination luring you down inappropriate byways. Yes, I agree that a surprise ending can be desirable, but that's a different matter from one that stupefies the reader because the novel wasn't leading in that direction, or not until very late on in the proceedings. You know from your own reading when a novel leaves you satisfied or when an author has botched it.

How many drafts?

Without a goal you risk floundering, writing thousands of words that ought to be torn up, once you have determined your ending, because they aren't the best route to it. Naturally, you will resist scrapping them, because none of us likes to waste work, and in themselves they are successful pieces of writing. So either you will try to smooth over the problems by editing, and hope for the best; or else you will throw away those scenes and plunge into a major rewrite. Honestly, it's far easier to decide what your goal is and kick straight at it.

There are writers, usually thriller writers, who claim they can only work in what I disparagingly dub the floundering method. They produce numerous drafts, making major alterations each time. But why bother when you can reach the same conclusions with no more effort than a little hard thinking? Like the majority of writers, my intention is always to do two drafts but occasionally I need three.

Your idea for a novel may have begun as baldly as the one about the woman in the cinema, but I would be very surprised if it's now devoid of a certain amount of plot and theme. Plot is the action in the story and theme is the subject, such as rivalry or the search for happiness. As our imaginative processes aren't compartmentalised, you can't concentrate on a story without seeing characters; or ruminate on the appearance and attitudes of your hero without picturing him doing something, or planning to. And if he's planning, then perhaps you've caught him scheming, and you've learned of that side of his nature. So the novel builds.

Inventing characters

Conjuring up characters is one of the most pleasurable parts of novel-making. Are you one of those writers whose idea for a whole book began with the appearance in your mind of an insistent character? Whether he came to you as a gift out of nowhere, or whether he's the result of a real effort to create him, you should pose some searching questions about him. They boil down to this: Is he strong enough? That doesn't mean he has to be physically or mentally robust, merely that he must be capable of interesting the reader for the length of the book. If he doesn't interest you, you can be certain he won't interest anyone else. How, then, can you develop him and ensure he's strong?

There's rather more to it than knowing the colour of his hair and whether he has a high-pitched giggle, although those details are important too. If he's based, however loosely, on a personal acquaintance or a man seen on television, you have a headstart because, in addition to his appearance, you will know something of his social background, the type of work he does and whether he speaks with a regional accent. Once you know a certain amount about a character you can try filling in details as though you were completing a questionnaire. Ask yourself, for instance, what car he drives, whether he drinks shorts or beer, whether he enjoys his own company or is lonely.

A profitable question is: 'Which newspaper does he read?' A newspaper often suggests a number of things about the person carrying it: his political standpoint, his level of education, whether he's a professional or a factory worker, whether he likes to consider a range of ideas or just wants opinions handed to him, whether he prefers classical music or pop, and so forth. While a newspaper is hardly an accurate guide to preoccupations and personality, it *is* an indicator and it works as a shorthand method of providing the reader with information about a character.

Ah, you can't work out which paper he reads. Well, perhaps you aren't familiar with what newspapers call their readership profiles. On the other hand, you may understand as well as I do the difference between a typical reader of the *Daily Telegraph* and one who takes the *Daily Star*. All right, your man is no newspaper reader. Now you have learned that.

Names

What is his name? When a name comes to you spontaneously it may suggest facets of a personality. Names can be tough, no nonsense names (Ian Fleming's James Bond; Adam Hall's Quiller), or soft ones (Dorothy Sayer's Peter Wimsey; Brian Freemantle's Charlie Muffin). The importance of names was summed up by Georges Simenon, that most intuitive of writers, who said:

> ❝ As soon as I name my main character I become him. It is not my intelligence that writes the novels but my impulses. ❞

When stuck for names, writers often turn to a gazeteer. Villages and towns have provided many a fictional hero's surname (Simon Brett's Charles Paris; Tim Heald's Simon Bognor). If you are setting your story in a particular part of the country you might like to use local place names. Once you have a surname, a first name usually suggests itself.

Motivation

Your protagonist can determine the form your novel takes. The obvious example is that if he's a policeman or a private eye, then you will shape a detective story. If he's not a good person, in the context of your story, you might write a crime novel from the criminal's perspective, and in that case the information you give about the investigation will be meagre. When he's neither the criminal nor the force for law and order, then his rôle may be less apparent. His motives will differ from those of the criminal or the person paid to investigate. Be clear about his reasons for becoming involved. He must justify his place at the centre of your novel.

On one level, you (and he) might believe he becomes involved because he wishes to carry out certain actions, and they set the story in motion or influence the way it develops. On another level, the reason might have more to do with his cast of mind than any actual details of the story, although he may remain unaware of this.

Say John is a car driver who notices men in a darkened layby lifting a box from a lorry into a car. Bored and under-occupied, which might mean either retired or unemployed, he spends an abnormal amount of time musing on what struck him as an obvious theft. A policeman hero could intervene and check what was going on. A private detective hero could be called in by the transport company to trail a lorry and end up hiding near the switchover layby to gather evidence. Those things aren't open to John. He broods, and he amuses himself by driving by in the hope of spotting a repetition. Soon he takes to hanging around there, fondling the mobile telephone he's bought ready to alert the police.

He sounds like a meddler, doesn't he? Incapable of achieving much himself, although it's doubtful he realises it, John is a man destined to get in the way. What if he fails to make the connection between the heavy box and the missing corpse? What if he's literally caught in the crossfire when armed police close in? What if he confuses the private detective and causes them both to fall into the hands of the gang? Whatever befalls John is going to seem like his own fault; and possibly, if fleetingly, to him.

Psychology

John is worthy of a place at the centre of a suspense novel: a figure who could recite sensible reasons for his behaviour, while reader and author know he has got it wrong. He's vulnerable, out of his depth and things are bound to end badly. John's story hangs on psychology. Novels of this kind are sometimes called psychological novels, or psychological suspense, yet all successful novels depend on psychology.

Although we have an instinctive understanding of the subjects, it pays writers to read a little psychology and psychiatry to help them root their fictional characters in typical human behaviour. Once you have grasped your hero's psychological make-up you have the key to how he thinks, what he's capable of and what he is not. It's no use asking more of John than he can perform. That isn't a failing of John, it's true of all characters, which is why you need to ask yourself whether the star of your novel is fit for the task ahead.

Liking the baddies

Writing in this genre you face a special hurdle. Your central character may be reprehensible, but it's your task to persuade decent readers to take to him and not close the book in disgust. In other kinds of fiction a writer invokes a reader's empathy for his protagonist by giving him attractive traits. But what on earth can you do with your brainchild who happens to be a psychopathic killer?

I faced this issue when I wrote *A Life of Adventure*, the novel that introduced Jim Rush, a bungling conman. My solution was to show him being considerate to an inadequate young man, Stefan, who comes to admire him. Until I had written a substantial part of the book, I didn't know that Stefan's admiration extended to keeping the clothes Jim discarded after a killing. In a sad attempt to protect Jim from a questioning police officer, Stefan dashes to his death on a railway line.

His death is a climax of the novel because of the chemistry between the two characters. It's shocking, but inevitable, that Stefan becomes another of Jim Rush's victims. Interestingly, women readers succumb to the charm Jim Rush is supposed to have for females in the novels, and they advance all manner of excuses for his behaviour. Men are appalled by him.

In contrast to my decision to give Jim Rush a redeeming feature, to coax the reader to keep company with him, there's the attitude of Los Angeles writer James Ellroy. He's an author of violent tales told in language hacked about like a strip cartoon, or indeed like some of his victims. Ellroy told an international conference of crime writers:

> ❝ I want the reader to empathise with the worst aspects of my characters. I'm writing for the voyeur in the reader. ❞

Violence, and the way you want the reader to respond to it, is another aspect of your novel to bear in mind while story and characters are developing. More about it in Chapter Four. Meanwhile, notice how it is handled by the authors you enjoy.

Setting

A setting for a novel can be anything, from a room in a flat to a whole island. Every location and building you use has to be fixed in the reader's mind. Mentioning a location by name is never enough, not even when it's as famous as London, which most readers will feel familiar with regardless that their impressions come entirely from television. London is immense and each district has its own characteristics.

What is required of the novelist is a flavour of the place that the characters know. This is achieved by describing what it looks like, conveying its atmosphere and illustrating what sort of people live there. No good handing the reader this information in a dollop, though. Weave it into the novel so that the picture grows as the narrative moves along.

You may give the heroine's first impressions of the shopping centre at Blankville, but not in a slab of sheer description that holds up the story. Build instead. The first time she sees it she's shocked by the neglect: slips of paper from the bank's cash machine are whirling in a draught from the door to the car park; plastic bottles are bobbing in a scummy fountain that isn't playing, anyway; sticky icecream wrappers are falling from an overflowing waste bin; there are no people, but there's all that whirling and bobbing and falling, of things that ought not to be. Next time she walks there, she pulls her collar up against the draught from the car park. The third time, a wrapper gets stuck to her shoe.

When you double back to pick up details in this way, you revive the initial scene and intensify the impression of Blankville shopping centre as an uncared-for, unattractive place where nothing good is going to happen. You may choose to set an important scene there late on in the story, the heroine no longer passing through but seeking something or confronting someone, perhaps being chased. Used efficiently, your setting will become an indispensable element of your novel. But if it's merely a backdrop, you have wasted it.

There's no harm in adopting a thoroughly practical attitude to the question of setting. Ask yourself whether you can truly afford to go to the tropical island you fancy using. Or whether you can get access to a particular site or building you need to become acquainted with. Doubtful? Then think again.

Some of us have a facility for catching the essence of a place in a few hours and a few words, others not. You may be more successful writing about a place you know than somewhere which strikes you as an exciting location. Be ready to change details, though. In *Evil Acts*, I installed a serial killer in a real house at the Angel, Islington, but I renamed the street and fudged a few details lest the real occupants of number 22 find my fictional flights distasteful. As the genre deals with nasty goings on, be cautious. At the least you could upset a few readers; at the worst you might be accused of libel.

——— Tempo, tone and theme ———

While you have been mulling over your story, your setting and the main characters, other things will have been sliding into place. Without working at it, you may have come to conclusions about tempo, tone and theme. **Tempo** means the pace at which you mean to tell the story. Of course, tempo varies during a novel, speeding up during thrilling scenes. This will probably be automatic: your own tension spurs you on and you notice you are using more active words and tenses, like dash*ing*. At one extreme, you might adopt a staccato overall tempo for your novel by opting for a snappy, clipped, way of writing, the sort popular for thrillers or hardboiled detective stories.

This is from *The Lady in the Lake* by Raymond Chandler, a writer whose hardboiled style is still being imitated half a century after he wrote it.

> ❡ I hardly heard what she said. It was like surf breaking beyond a point, out of sight. The gun had my interest.
>
> I broke the magazine out. It was empty. I turned the gun and looked into the breach. That was empty too. I sniffed the muzzle. It reeked.
>
> I dropped the gun into my pocket. A six shot .25-calibre automatic. Emptied out. Shot empty, and not too long ago. But not in the last half-hour either. ❡

It wouldn't be impossible to take a languorous approach, lulling the reader and making the shocks therefore more shocking when they arrive. But alarm results in agitation and urgent activity, and tempo increases, sentences becoming shorter and sharper, and vocabulary changing to blunter language. When you grow tense, so does your writing.

This is from the first chapter of *In a Lonely Place,* a 1950 suspense novel with a California setting, by Dorothy B. Hughes.

> ❡ She had just passed over the mid hump, she was on the final stretch of down grade. Walking fast. But as he reached that section, a car turned at the corner below, throwing its blatant light up on her, on him. Again anger plucked at his face; his steps slowed. The car speeded up the Incline, passed him, but the damage was done, the darkness had broken. As if it were a parade, the stream of cars followed the first car, scratching their light over the path and the road and the high earthen Palisades across. The girl was safe; he could feel the relaxation in her footsteps. Anger beat him like a drum. ❡

The **tone** of a novel may be described in words like comic, wry, reflective, tongue-in-cheek, bittersweet, or in compounds such as incipient fear, sense of lurking evil and sense of unease. Tempo may be the result of conscious decision-making, because you can choose what pace of storytelling you wish to aim at. Tone is likely to be dictated by your material. As in everything, there are exceptions. A comic crime novel could emerge from the blackest tale should the writer choose.

Theme is one of those words that frightens writers, and not only beginners. They fret that they don't know from the earliest stage of planning a novel what their theme is to be. If, on the other hand, they are confident from the outset that it is, for instance, *disappointment*, they worry that half way through the novel they have discovered it's actually *loss*. Theme is presented as an obstacle to be overcome before pen touches paper. How can you invent a story, develop characters, choose your setting and discuss tone and tempo, when you don't know what the theme is? Luckily, the truth is that theme is one of the aspects of a novel that you needn't fuss about. It will turn up on its own.

There are writers whose starting point for a novel is theme. Perhaps they have an urge to write a book about exodus, disgrace or revenge. They will develop a story suitable to treat their chosen theme, and they will conjure up characters to fit. But for other writers, novels come together in the mind without us taking solemn decisions about each element. Because you don't know what the theme of a story is, it doesn't follow that it's lacking.

The little people

Beginners often worry about the handling of minor characters, how many people a novel needs, and whether a writer ought to be acquainted with them all before starting off. The number depends on the type of story you are working on. A crime novel involving an investigation may require far more than others. Your investigator will have a client; there will be a corpse; and a series of people, some of whom will become suspects, plus their cohorts, who are encountered during the enquiry. For another sort of book, only a handful may be wanted. There are no optimum numbers for different kinds of novel but you ought to resist using any characters that aren't strictly necessary, because you will be asking the reader to remember each and every one.

If you suspect, while planning or writing, that you have too many, consider dropping some. Your solution may be to amalgamate the happy gang in the neighbouring house into one bright and bouncy teenager; and to refer to her friends but keep them offstage. Minor characters will come to mind while you are writing, yet you have to remain in charge. There is room in the darkest crime novel for touches of light relief, but over-indulge in the antics of the happy crew next door and you weaken your novel. They will become too prominent and their every appearance will slow the tempo and lighten the tone. You don't want that, do you? Get tough with them.

Readers readily grasp family relationships, so when Gladys turns up again after ten chapters' absence, the slightest nudge from the author is enough for them to recall that she's Celia's aunt who went to Brighton the day after the murder. But when you are using a wider setting, perhaps a network of colleagues, they are harder for the reader to distinguish. Unfortunately, it's all too easy to mar a novel by failing to clarify minor characters.

Make each one memorable when he's introduced. A quirk of personality could be mentioned, or a physical detail, and these points referred to on subsequent occasions. Maybe the hero is struck by the fact that a smartly dressed woman has neglected to clean her shoes, and he recalls this when he thinks about her later.

Rubbing along together

It's very important that you understand, and impart to the reader, the way the people in your cast relate to each other. Yes, you should know Clive's fears and weaknesses, his bad habits and good impulses, but you should also be aware that he grates on Jeremy and Anthony distrusts him. Although you know, broadly, what your story is, your characters are your tools for telling it. Their relationships will result in the page by page detail that grows into a novel.

Some of them may have their own, lesser, stories running alongside your main one. Writing, for instance, about homelessness, you could have your principal character fighting eviction from a squat, while a couple of the minor characters are struggling to pay their mortgage, and someone else has inherited a house. Novels in which the stories of major and minor characters are variations on a theme are called symphonic.

An efficient way to confuse the reader is to use names that are similar. Having once produced a first draft in which nearly everyone's name began with W, I now take the precaution of listing names as I invent characters. This tally also sends off alarm bells before numbers get out of hand.

— How long is this thing going on? —

One of the commonest questions writers are asked is: 'How long does it take to write a novel?'. We give differing answers because we measure in various ways, but really they are largely bogus. Thriller writers, for instance, established a fashion for claiming to work set hours at a desk for a certain number of weeks. They totted up and announced that it took, say, three months to write a novel. Probe, though, and you discover they didn't include time devoted to developing the idea.

Patricia Highsmith, equal to Simenon as a writer of suspense fiction, said that anything from six months to three years might pass while her germ of an idea developed to the stage where she felt able to begin plotting. Before she was ready to invent a plot, she needed to be extremely familiar with her characters, knowing far more about them than ever appeared in print, and also absolutely clear about the setting.

Three years spent pondering the characters sounds like a major problem, especially for the writer who plans to make a living as a novelist, but fortunately novelists are able to overlap. While letting a future novel simmer in the mind, they will be happily writing a current one, dealing with editor's queries on the most recently delivered manuscript, and possibly making public appearances to publicise a book that has just been published.

———— Testing your ideas ————

Highsmith's novels came to her in this order: character, setting and, trailing a long way behind, plot. If you are lucky, the elements arrive more or less together, one thing leading to another. A setting such as a villa in Tuscany tends to suggest a middle-class family of English holidaymakers, plus a concierge and one or two other locals. The story might hinge on conflict, or at any rate competition, between the holidaymakers and the locals. One or other group has a guilty secret which, our subject being crime, includes a murder.

Supposing the striking character who has caught your eye is a down-and-out selling the *Big Issue* on the streets of London, the setting is bound to be the rough underside of the city: hostels for the homeless, mentally ill people sleeping in the streets, and drug addicts. Your novel can contain as many shades of crime as you care to pack in.

Perhaps a plot has turned up first. An elderly couple are slaughtered on a remote Scottish farm, and their son is falsely accused because he's assumed to be after an inheritance. While hiding from the police, he discovers the killers.

When it looks too easy

When characters, setting and story come to you very easily, it's worth wondering whether it might not have been suspiciously smooth. Inspiration is a blessing, but are you being facile? First ideas should always be challenged. If they are good, scrutiny won't damage them. When they don't pass muster, you will save yourself much effort and disappointment.

Pangs of doubt about that set-up in Tuscany? Don't despair, improve. Make it a shade less predictable. Might the holidaymakers become more interesting? Not a family but a gathering of another kind, with secrets to match? And that concierge... rather a caricature, wasn't she? Then make her more individual.

Then there's that fellow with the *Big Issue*. He's vivid but is he truly as inarticulate as you are making out? Used as the protagonist, his inadequacies could prove a hindrance as you move the story along. So who is he really? A graduate researching life on the rough side? An undercover policeman from the drugs squad? A lottery winner gone to ground to dodge beggars? All right, they aren't all sensible thoughts and neither will yours be, but don't let that stop you having them. When there's a fundamental weakness, you will be glad you spotted it.

Think now about the novel in your head. You have a good deal of the story, or you know about central characters, or perhaps both. You know whether the setting is a certain town or house, or a marina or a holiday island, or what you will. At this stage of a novel my notes are littered with 'perhaps', 'possibly', 'maybe' and 'might'. All words indicating doubt and potential. On the other hand, what I am definite about is the feeling I want a story to have. I mean for the characters in it. Words like 'claustrophobic', 'hopeless' and 'trapped' crop up. Try asking yourself how your characters feel. You may discover that this is something else you already know about your novel.

When characters are stuck at the Tuscan villa, or in a similar situation, holiday lightheartedness could give way to a sense of claustrophobia, regardless of the endless vistas through the window. The *Big Issue* seller might be battling gamely against terrible odds, but as they are indeed terrible odds the pervading feeling of that book might excusably be one of hopelessness. A young man gone to ground amidst accusations of double murder is an excellent candidate for feeling trapped. But, once again, those are the obvious answers and perhaps they aren't the most interesting ones.

By the most interesting I don't mean the most eccentric. Yes, this is a balancing act. You are discouraged from being banal but you are also being warned off being outlandish. The middle ground is where successful novels thrive. Characters may be allotted sufficient foibles to let them shine as individuals, and stories may benefit from featuring predictable situations reversed, but none of this should go so far that the reader doesn't believe a word. The effect of crime and suspense fiction is achieved by the reader sharing the anxieties of certain characters, and if he can't believe in them or accept their predicaments, then the novel fails.

When a reader opens a novel, it's a declaration that he's willing to collude with the author: he will suspend disbelief and let the writer guide him through a fictional world. He puts his trust in you and, although he knows it's 'only fiction', he will cringe when your hero is thumped, and sigh when your heroine is sad, and when you make a little joke upon the page he will smile. But he is no fool. He has lived as you have lived and he knows when you are telling the truth about human beings. When you are not, he becomes impatient. He decides the characters you have introduced him to aren't responding as real people respond, or that your story is impossible. He closes the book.

—— **Working on your novel 2** ——

If you worked on your story after Chapter One now concentrate on character, and vice versa.

Central character

1 Write a description, as fully as you like, of the central character, protagonist or hero in your novel. Can you answer these questions about him?

- What is his physical appearance? As well as build and features, notice whether he's neat or untidy in his dress.
- What sort of voice does he have?

- How does he walk? A loping stride? Shambling? You get clues to character from the way a person moves.
- How does he relate to other characters?
- Which newspaper does he read?
- Is he going to end up a winner or a loser, and which does he habitually do?

Or:

1 If you worked on character last time now make notes on the story you are planning to use. Don't forget to record the source of any information, possibly a book or a newspaper cutting. You may wish to look through the original at a later point, to ensure you have made significant changes and disguised real people.

2 Reduce the story to its bones and pinpoint where the conflict lies.

3 Encapsulate the story in a paragraph. Keep it to one page.

4 Decide whether you feel it has the makings of a suspense novel, a detective novel or a crime novel of another type.

5 Test how fully you understand the story by seeing whether you can answer these key questions about it: who, what, where, when, why and how?

Or:

1 If you still don't have a story or a character in mind, write about what you do know so far. The setting?

Reading list

Raymond Chandler, *The Lady in the Lake.*
James Ellroy, *American Tabloid.*
Lesley Grant-Adamson, *The Face of Death.*
Dorothy B. Hughes, *In a Lonely Place.*
Georges Simenon, *Maigret Afraid.*

3

WAYS AND MEANS

Literature is a luxury; fiction is a necessity.   G.K. Chesterton

When writers and critics of literary fiction decided, during the seventies, that novels were better off without stories, they deterred many would be novelists who had expected to join the mainstream. Stranded, these novices cast an eye over genre fiction and a goodly number turned to crime. The result was an influx of talent producing fine novels and attracting yet more writers to the genre. People began to murmur about a new Golden Age in crime fiction, to rival the one that flourished between the two World Wars.

Although the literary novel eventually rediscovered the merits of the story, it soon became confessional. Writers began to explore their own relationships and personalities, exposing themselves and in a manner which most of us resist. Writing genre fiction excuses us from doing that. We draw on our experiences, yes, but our novels aren't overtly autobiographical.

Two sorts of people are currently writing crime fiction. There are the legions, and they are predominantly writers of the detective story, who would have chosen it, anyway. And there are those who see themselves primarily as novelists who just happen to be writing within the bounds of a genre. Cross-fertilisation between the two camps has been entirely beneficial. Boundaries dividing crime from literary fiction have been pushed back, and critics accord the genre a higher status.

The long shadow of Agatha Christie, doubtless forever to be called the Queen of Crime, still falls across us but it's fading at last because there can be hardly anyone who fails to appreciate that her work doesn't epitomise crime fiction, merely one variety.

Traditions and trends

There's another way of categorising British crime writers these days. While most are writing in the British tradition, an increasing number of the younger ones are influenced by the American. There are no sheep and goats here, just two rich traditions to plunder. It's broadly true that British novelists concentrate on social issues and a quest for justice, whereas Americans are fascinated by psychological and metaphysical problems. Fatal passion is a popular theme in American crime novels, and their detectives validate the myth of personal integrity in a corrupt world.

This is one of the hackneyed questions asked about the genre: 'Why are the women writers so much better than the men?' It crops up in interviews as well as private conversations. My answer is that it isn't entirely true, and that the standard of writing is generally high. But there's no escaping the fact that women have always been top of the tree, and that it's their work over the last fifteen years that has led to claims of a new Golden Age. They have indeed breathed new life into the genre.

I don't see any mystery. The reason is feminism. Because women's lives changed radically, so did the fictional women we write about. Heroines who are strong, independent creatures are credible creations these days, and they are free to have the kinds of adventures once reserved for heroes. Art is happily imitating life, and the readers are delighted.

Defining the categories

Time, now, for me to define crime and suspense fiction. These are personal definitions, arrived at after discussion with numerous writers and publishers but also backed by my experience of writing several kinds. Another writer, or a book shop assistant stocking shelves, might label them slightly differently but that would be no surprise because novels don't conform to exact formulae. It doesn't matter if you jib at the way I have done it since I am not sending you shopping, only offering a guide to the possible methods of telling your story.

The structure of your novel will be determined by the type you decide to write. As you read through the definitions, you will probably realise that your story seems especially suited to one form. But perhaps you find yourself havering. In that case, you will have to pin down exactly what final effect you hope to achieve. Up until now it has been valuable to think about your novel in the broadest terms, so that you retained the flexibility to develop your story in whichever direction appeared most promising. Before you get embroiled in detailed plotting and planning, you need to become more precise.

——— Classic detective stories ———

The classic English detective story, or *whodunit*, is a short, taut account of a murder investigation by a police officer, private detective or amateur sleuth. The writer observes certain conventions in the telling, most importantly providing the reader with every clue the detective uses to solve the case. Favourite settings are fictional villages or provincial towns, although there's a current vogue for using real ones. Detectives may be either amateur sleuths, private detectives or police officers.

Traditionally, the whodunit begins with a murder disrupting the comfortable lives of a group of middle- or upper-class people. Then comes an investigation during which everyone's failings are revealed. But once the detective names the culprit, that act in itself appears sufficient to put everything right. Punishment doesn't matter, only the truth. It's axiomatic that the guilty party is named and everyone else, including the reader, is reassured.

Literary critics have been fascinated by the whodunit. Brigid Brophy wrote that:

❝ The detective does the Ego's work: making sense of the irrational and acquitting us of blood guilt. ❞

And W.H. Auden explained:

❝ The rôle of the detective is less to prove the guilt of the murderer than the innocence of all other characters. The murderer is a scapegoat whose expulsion redeems the Edenic community and reassures the reader of the externality of guilt to world and self. ❞

Whodunits have an impeccable pedigree, coming to us through a chain of eminent writers including Sir Arthur Conan Doyle who created Sherlock Holmes and his helper, Dr Watson; Agatha Christie who invented the amateur Miss Marple and also the police inspector Hercule Poirot and his assistant, Hastings; and Dorothy L. Sayers who dreamed up Lord Peter Wimsey.

One can describe stories from the Golden Age, and not unfairly, as puzzles on a page. Writers contrived ingenious methods of murder, and blessed their detectives with flashes of brilliance bright enough to illuminate the truth. Having created a sharp-witted and probably paternalistic detective, few writers of the period bothered to develop the other characters, or to make effective use of setting, or to spare a thought for anything but plot, plot, plot. Above all, they avoided questioning society's values. The mystery was all.

The best of these old stories remain popular today. Side by side, detective and reader continue to hoover up the clues and draw logical conclusions. To be fair, it was impossible to develop character without undermining the premise that any one of the suspects might be culpable.

In his famous Decalogue, published in the preface to *Best Detective Stories of 1928–29*, Ronald Knox urged detective story writers to obey ten rules. They were:

1 The criminal must be someone mentioned in the early part of the story, but must not be anyone whose thoughts the reader has been allowed to follow.

2 All supernatural or preternatural agencies are ruled out as a matter of course.

3 Not more than one secret room or passage is allowable.

4 No hitherto undiscovered poisons may be used, nor any appliance which will need a long explanation at the end.

5 No Chinaman must figure in the story.

6 No accident must ever help the detective, nor must he ever have an unaccountable intuition which proves to be right.

7 The detective must not himself commit the crime.

8 The detective must not light on any clues which are not instantly produced for the inspection of the reader

9 The Stupid Friend of the detective, the Watson, must not conceal any thoughts which pass through his mind; his intelligence must be slightly, but very slightly, below that of the average reader.

10 Twin brothers, and doubles generally, must not appear unless we have been duly prepared for them.

Knox wasn't inventing all those rules, he was codifying in an attempt to curb excesses that threatened to make the detective story laughable. Writers responded, which was a good thing insofar as they were agreeing to play fair with the puzzle-solving reader. It meant though, that the form became static: experimentation led to accusations of cheating.

John Dickson Carr, *The Hollow Man*.
Agatha Christie, *The Mysterious Affair at Styles*.
Conan Doyle, *The Speckled Band*.
Cyril Hare, *Tragedy at Law*.
Dorothy L. Sayers, *Gaudy Night*.

Non fiction

W.H. Auden, *The Guilty Vicarage*.
Colin Watson, *Snobbery with Violence*.

———— Modern crime novels ————

When we talk about the modern English crime novel we are referring to a whole spectrum of novels. At one end are those whose origins in the classic detective story are obvious. At the other extreme are novels that involve no detection whatsoever, and are distinguished from mainstream fiction purely by the fact that they centre on a crime. Social issues and the quest for justice are the usual concerns of the modern crime novel. Detective stories continue to reassure, although less confidently than once upon a time.

Those that aren't, even loosely, tales of detection may be written from the point of view of the criminal or someone less closely involved in the crime, or from several conflicting points of view. The joy of the modern crime novel is its flexibility in the hands of an imaginative writer. If you are going to write one, your deepest interest is probably not the mystery and its unravelling, because you may be using the form as a framework on which to hang your story about a social problem or a place that you feel the urge to write about. Perhaps you want to take an historical murder case and re-examine it in the course of a novel; or you have a mind to explore what happens to a child growing up in the wake of a crime; or you have opinions about the pressures of modern life which tempt people into criminality. Anything goes, as long as you ensure a crime is the core of the novel. After that, the choice is yours.

The borderline between suspense fiction and crime novels about, say, the child growing up in the wake of a crime or people's circumstances tempting them into illegalities, is hazy indeed but this matters not. Two writers tackling the same topic could well produce novels that fell on opposite sides of the boundary. One author might find during the writing that he was giving such scant attention to the actual crime that, instead of it being at the core of the book as he had intended, it was diminished to a painful memory that influenced his characters' decisions at key points in their lives. Meanwhile the other author might have his characters obsessed with the crime, digging into the past to clarify it or choosing to perpetuate its effects, and keeping the incident at the centre of their lives and, therefore, of the book.

Detective novels

The whodunit, as it reappears under the heading of modern crime fiction, is justifiably called the detective novel. Rules are relaxed although the basic principles of a murder plus a successful investigation apply. It is a more spacious and profound book that allows the author to study predicaments and personalities. Unlike its predecessor it is concerned with theme. While the classic is about order disrupted and eventually restored, the detective novel knows few certainties, and writers make the point that to understand the whole truth about anything is impossible. By the final page the sleuth will know, or believe he knows, the identity of the killer. When the story has been told from more than one viewpoint, the reader may be aware that the sleuth is wrong.

The detective novel which stays closest to its classical origins retains the challenge a writer throws down to a reader. 'Can you work out whodunit before I tell you?' We continue to hand over the clues, both false and genuine ones. Our detective usually has a colleague or confidant, who may be of considerable help to him but is invaluable to the writer who can lighten the text with their discussions instead of having the hero running over things in his head all the time. But there are two significant changes from the way these stories were written in the past. We seldom pretend now that rooting out the killer makes everything all right again. Instead we show people damaged by the experience. And the stories aren't unremittingly middle or upper class.

A typical one of recent years would be set in a fictitious town and feature a police officer who copes with a murder enquiry while also wrangling with a subordinate whose opinions of society, and therefore of the other characters, differ from his own. (Ruth Rendell's Wexford and Burden; Colin Dexter's Morse and Lewis.) Depending on his temperament and social background, our hero may either take a wry look at society or else feel dismayed by it; but it's hardly his rôle to undermine it, any more than his forerunner in the classic stories did.

As suspects no longer need to be physically together, for instance in a country house, they are linked in subtler ways. (Sheila Radley put them on the same postman's round in *Death on the Happy Highway*). All are introduced to the reader early on. (My method in *Patterns in the Dust* was to open with the foxhunt holding the first meet of the season in the village square, a time when locals gather.) There's a scattering of clues, some that will eventually put the detective on to the killer. Also there are false clues, called red herrings, designed to mislead detective and reader but calculated to expose other characters' guilty secrets. Thus suspicion falls on a series of suspects until the detective homes in on his quarry. Then comes the dénouement when all is explained.

A lengthy dénouement is, I think, a weakness because the pace flags. The way detective stories used to be written, the dénouement was what happened when the action came to a stop. Readers and characters together entered the library to be offered the solution, with the detective highlighting each clue and explaining his reasoning. We no longer permit the accusing detective publicly to turn his scorn and scrutiny on one suspect after another before exonerating them, until there's only the murderer left.

But phony as it was, the traditional library confrontation was dramatic. Now we face the anticlimax of the detective giving a meandering recital of the case to a colleague, which is realistic but dull. The ideal is to weave the story together in such a way that it doesn't come juddering to a halt to make way for a dénouement. Keep the action going while truths are exposed and characters respond to them, and keep at least one strand of the narrative in play right up to the end. The fewer words written after the truth is unveiled, the greater the climax and the crisper the novel.

Detective heroes of all types – police, private detectives, amateurs; male or female – now routinely have self-doubts, friends, families, pets,

marital problems, love affairs, awkward colleagues and larky neighbours. Putting characters into context makes them seem more like real
people, but the writer risks growing self-indulgent and focusing too
often on home life and menagerie instead of concentrating on the plot.
It may take an effort of will to deny your hero an extra gerbil but,
unless superfluous gerbils are germane to the plot, it's an effort to be
recommended. Although *you* might be enchanted by your hero's weakness for furry little creatures, your readers will know it's padding.

Anthea Fraser, *The April Rainers.*
Michael Gilbert, *Smallbone Deceased.*
Caroline Graham, *The Killings at Badger's Drift.*
Sheila Radley, *Death on the Happy Highway.*
Andrew Taylor, *Blood Relation.*
June Thomson, *Death Cap.*

Police procedurals

Confusingly, two contrasting types of novel are referred to in Britain
as police procedurals because they are both concerned with the way
the police operate. One variety is the police detective novel, which
grew out of the classic detective story; and the other belongs to an
American tradition and is less popular with British writers. To create
either you require a knowledge of police work, but this isn't difficult
to come by. There are books on the subject and each police region has
helpful public relations officers.

American-inspired police procedurals centre on a police station and a
team of colleagues. They are shaped like picaresque novels, by which
I mean that a series of interesting characters appear on the scene, act
out their dramas and are gone. The authors' underlying purposes are
to examine the methods used by the police to investigate crime and to
show how the clubby, male, world of the police operates.

Police work being largely routine, the novels are enlivened by empha-
sising the private lives and working relationships of the team. They
are realistic, insofar as cases aren't always satisfactorily concluded
and policemen don't always behave impeccably. Usually these novels
are written in series, with characters evolving from story to story as
they do in television series such as *Hill Street Blues.* (Ed McBain's
87th Precinct novels show you how it should be done.)

If you are proposing to write an American-style police procedural, your police station will benefit from being in a town big enough to allow for a range of crime and various social classes. Whether you are using a real town or conjuring one up, you should aim to give the reader a definite flavour of the place. Inevitably, you will be juggling a lot of characters, all of whom must be easily distinguished.

Police procedurals – whichever variety you fancy writing, the name contains a warning. When the police conduct a murder investigation there are set procedures to be followed. To produce a credible novel you need to know exactly how they go about their affairs, and in the specific area where you are setting your story. It isn't enough to understand how the Metropolitan Police behave in London if you are using a provincial force. By checking up you can avoid ruinous mistakes.

Some things you may choose to fudge, but let them be deliberate decisions rather than blunders. When writing the American-style police procedural, you can accommodate a two-week gap in the investigation while a laboratory tests samples which the Scene of Crimes Officer gathered near the body. Feel free to fill the gap by passing on news from the family front. Has the SOCO's wife run off with the car park attendant? Or opened a sandwich bar? Or been caught shoplifting? Here's your chance to say so. But in the more usual police detective story, which I am calling the English one, undue waffling about Detective Inspector Wizard's family won't suffice.

Nor will it do to pretend there was no queue at the laboratory and the forensic scientists rushed the job. In real life it probably takes the full two weeks to grow the cultures or whatever else they had to do, and should you know of a quicker way then the police would love to hear from you. Your best course is to find out the time routinely required for various tests and, when planning your novel, allow for it. A story that hinges on the results of DNA tests can't be completed within a timescale of one week as tests (currently) take between one week and a fortnight.

By the way, there is more than one method of testing for DNA. Originally blood samples were taken but now laboratories may work with epithelial cells scraped from the inner wall of the cheek, or with at least ten hairs, plus roots, plucked from any part of the body, except pubic, nominated by the donor.

When there's no logical solution to your timing problem, you may shrug it off by being vague about the exact number of days that pass during the telling of your story. Cut, for instance, from one aspect of the investigation to another, and pick up the thread once the results of the test are to hand. The one thing you can't afford is to bring the action to a standstill.

Michael Dibdin, *Ratking*.
John Harvey, *Cold Light*.
Reginald Hill, *Dead Heads*.
Tony Hillerman, *A Thief of Time*.
Ed McBain, *Cop Hater*.
Hillary Waugh, *Last Seen Wearing...*

Private detectives

The same goes for your private detective: you need to learn how the real ones operate in the country you are writing about. In Britain, they are no more allowed to run around waving firearms than you and I are. Much of their work lacks drama: they keep watch for shoplifters; check up on errant husbands and wives; hunt for people who have gone missing; and track down any information their clients can't find out for themselves. For the purposes of fiction your detective must become involved in a murder, and you will have to contrive a way. In old-fashioned detective stories it wasn't unheard of for a stumped police officer to send for a private detective to solve a case for him. Please don't be tempted.

You ought to be clear about your private detective's motivation because it will influence his behaviour. He isn't put on this earth to investigate murders, that's the prerogative of the police. Therefore he might be delving into the case because a relative of the victim is unhappy with the official investigation, or else because he has a personal interest in it, or for some other valid reason. Hired by a relative, he's doing a paid job and that will be enough for him to stick at it. With a personal interest, he may not be paid but will be fired up by his own eagerness to get to the bottom of the mystery.

The private detective operates outside the system and offers you different opportunities from the policeman. He – and increasingly she – may be anarchic, angry at an unfair world and glad not to have much of a stake in it. There isn't too much risk of other members of your cast finding him paternalistic. He can be as tough and mean as you like, but there is a proviso. Never forget that he has to be sufficiently sympathetic for people to trust him with their secrets, and also reliable about doing the job.

Liza Cody, *Head Case*.
Lesley Grant-Adamson, *Flynn*.
P.D. James, *An Unsuitable Job for a Woman*.
Dan Kavanagh, *Fiddle City*.
Julie Smith, *Tourist Trap*.

——— Hardboiled detective fiction ———

This term has long been applied to American stories about macho characters who make their living as private detectives. At the time they originated, the police weren't trusted and the private investigator had become a fact of life in the USA. Typically, the fictional hero was a cynical loner, an alienated man who had evolved his own code of honour. With corruption all around, he felt free to use violence to counter it. He was, in effect, the cowboy hero brought in from the Wild West and given an office in town.

Appropriately, in view of the fellow's anti-establishment status, the stories lacked the tight plotting that marked the English classic detective story of the same period. Often they were composed by stringing together a series of interviews. Another major difference was that they fell short of novel length.

Their effect, though, was wonderfully energetic. Heroes were blessed with fantastic physical courage, spattered the pages with witticisms, dispatched villains in scenes of vivid violence, and were swaggeringly beholden to no one. Dashiel Hammet is credited with starting it off and Raymond Chandler with perfecting it, but hordes of American writers have written hardboiled ever since. The news is that the gumshoe is on the other foot. Tough gals are currently walking the mean streets, too.

Distinctions have blurred since those early days, and it's no longer a sensible generalisation that all the energetic writing comes from one side of the Atlantic and all the better crafted novels are written on the other. But what does persist is the British concern with form and the American inclination to bounce the story along in a reckless fashion from one startling incident to the next. In the last few years a number of British writers have opted to write hardboiled. Exponents believe they are refashioning British crime fiction, but it's more likely that their experiments will add yet another strand to an already rich tradition.

Writing a hardboiled detective story is akin to writing a thriller. Pace is frenetic, narration is staccato, and your average hero is a man in a hurry, not one to wait upon events. He is a memorable character with a taste in cars or clothes that make him stand out from the herd. The book is all go – no time for musing when the pages can be sparkling with dialogue.

Ah, dialogue. The rule is for fizzing exchanges, and this is where Americans score because their demotic speech is so colourful. Chandler set a standard for humorous, figurative speech and writers still inject that element into their books. But too much of it is wearing and, besides, one reader's witticism is another reader's facetious remark. Comic writing is always tricky. Even if you have a gift for it, don't overdo the funny stuff because it reduces tension.

Urban hero

The hardboiled detective story is fundamentally an urban one. Unlike other detective heroes, but rather like thriller heroes, the man may be capable of enacting crimes as appalling as the ones he sets out to investigate. In these books the pattern is that his incompetence gets him into trouble and if the easiest solution is to kill someone, he does. Basically, the stories are about his endeavours to extricate himself from the mess. No happy endings: the results of his investigation may be disastrous for him and everyone involved. If you write one of these, avoid killing him off because he might have the makings of a series hero.

More don'ts. Don't let your hero be violent for the sake of violence. Don't make him a hopeless loser. Don't deny him any redeeming qualities. Your purpose is to enthral your reader, not alienate or depress him.

American
Raymond Chandler, *Farewell My Lovely*.
Dashiell Hammet, *The Maltese Falcon*.
Sara Paretsky, *Burn Marks*.

British
Sarah Dunant, *Birth Marks*.
Bill James, *Halo Parade*.

The amateur sleuth

Amateur sleuths are an attractive proposition because they have even fewer restraints than the private detective and you can use a background you already know. Yes, but this brings me to what I call the Perceptive Barber Syndrome. You may write a satisfactory novel about a barber who notices odd goings on, downs his soap and razor and sets off to investigate. This is all right for one book, but suppose you are asked to write a series about him? Publishers of whodunits crave series characters but how plausible is it that he makes a habit of hanging up the closed sign and flitting off to play amateur detective? Do assess the limitations of your hero before you plunge in. An amateur who is in a natural position to investigate, someone like a journalist or an insurance investigator, has better scope.

When I was inventing Rain Morgan I originally imagined her as the news editor of a provincial paper, a job I had myself enjoyed. On second thoughts I transferred her to Fleet Street as a gossip columnist. No longer deskbound, she had been granted the freedom to travel and encounter people in all corners of society. In the series that followed, the frothy world of the gossip column provided a foil to the topical social issues Rain was obliged to face when stories for the paper turned to murder. As a news editor, she could have done no more than send others out into the fray.

There's a myth that detective stories are easy to churn out. It's only true if you have a special bent for them. Writers who enjoy the challenge of working within the conventions may become prolific authors. Hordes of others fail wretchedly. You have a promising start as an admirer of the genre who reads analytically, attending to the way the author constructs them and teases you along. By respecting the conventions, and shaping your story accordingly, you can create the framework. Then it's up to you to flesh out the characters until they seem real people doing reasonable things, rather than counters being moved around a board to satisfy the demands of the plot.

Liza Cody, *Bucketnut.*
Lesley Grant-Adamson, *Wild Justice.*
Jessica Mann, *Funeral Sites.*
Mike Phillips, *Blood Rights.*
Annette Roome, *A Second Shot in the Dark.*
Joan Smith, *A Masculine Ending.*

─────── Comic detective stories ───────

Comic detective stories tend to be pastiches of the real thing. The comedy depends on characters going about their business in a serious fashion, unaware that the situation they are in is ludicrous. The result should be hilarious but a fast tempo is needed to bring it off.

Comic writing of all kinds is more difficult to sell, which may account for the low output of these stories. The *Crime Writers' Association* encourages them with an annual award, the cause of much amusement when it was bestowed on Nancy Livingston who confessed she hadn't intended her book to be funny. It is, though, and so are the other adventures of Mr. Pringle.

Simon Brett, *Star Trap.*
H.R.F. Keating, *Inspector Ghote Trusts the Heart.*
Nancy Livingston, *Trouble at Acquitaine.*
Mike Ripley, *Just another Angel.*
Leslie Thomas, *Dangerous Davies.*
Colin Watson, *Whatever's Been Going on at Mumblesby?*

─────── Historical crime ───────

The fascination of writing this type of novel lies in creating a story appropriate to its period, and then bringing that period alive for the reader. Some writers look no further than their own childhoods, to days whose memory shines brightest. Kingsley Amis harked back to the thirties for his version of the Golden Age detective story, complete with victim staggering in through the french windows.

Others research the early days of policing or forensic science to furnish their Victorian detective stories, and Ellis Peters went all the way back to the twelfth century for Brother Cadfael. Everything in these books, which the Americans call history mysteries, depends on research. Unlike other novels, where it's normal to do part of the research as you write and the story continues to unfold, writers of historical crime say they research their period first and then invent a story that allows them to use what they have learned.

Apart from novels set wholly in the past there's the type epitomised by Josephine Tey's *The Daughter of Time*, where a present-day character unravels an historical mystery.

Lindsey Davis, *Venus in Copper.*
Colin Dexter, *The Wench is Dead.*
Umberto Eco, *The Name of the Rose.*
Peter Lovesey, *The False Inspector Dew.*
Ellis Peters, *A Morbid Taste for Bones.*
Josephine Tey, *The Daughter of Time.*

Noir

This is lowlife at its murkiest. The cast list for a noir novel may include prostitutes, gangsters, drug dealers and other losers who exist on the margins of society. Characters are bitterly anarchic, the language is fierce, and physical violence erupts frequently. But for all the freedoms noir grabs, the result is usually stylised. Some writers of noir claim theirs is the only fiction that faithfully reflects society; but other exponents declare they are deliberately writing a modern urban fantasy.

Noir became a cult in the early nineties, the decade that saw the death of the leading British writer Derek Raymond. As its name suggests, it has long had a following in France. Walter Mosley is applauded for his use of American black vernacular in his series about Easy Rawlins.

Alex Abella, *The Killing of the Saints.*
Walter Mosley, *A Red Death.*
Derek Raymond, *I Was Dora Suarez.*

Suspense

The principal of 'let 'em laugh, let 'em cry, let 'em wait' sums up suspense fiction, even though laughter is normally reduced to the occasional smile at irony or wit. These novels can be as dark and brooding as the author feels the subject demands, and a grim humour will suffice. Character in decay is a familiar theme. Crime, or the aftermath of it, is usually involved but this isn't a perquisite. Without straying into crime, horror, thrillers or ghost stories you may produce a creditable suspense novel.

The suspense novel may be defined by the things it doesn't have to do. It doesn't, for example, have to offer reassurance, as the detective story does when the killer's identity is revealed. Neither does it have to involve crime, nor are there conventions to follow. It can be a quiet book, lacking the dash and flurry that peps up crime novels and especially thrillers. No particular length is required. In fact, the freedoms it confers are as wide as you wish to make them. Key elements are the study of character, and an engrossing story which contains a degree of mystery and is told in a manner that raises tension and keeps it high until the final page.

A typical story allows the reader to watch unwitting characters plodding towards their doom. This business of knowing that something frightful is going to happen yet being unable to tear oneself away is a basic human trait and it lies at the root of storytelling. Think of the fairy tales that we listen to over and over because of that tremendous narrative pull. We fully understand there's going to be an accident, and we are determined to be in the accident crowd.

Novels in which the name of the killer is known from the outset are referred to as whydunits because they examine the reasons for a crime. These reasons lie in the character of an individual, and the novel peels away the layers until the truth is plain. Whydunits have become popular and it's often supposed that they are an innovation. Indeed not. The first of them, Francis Iles's *Malice Aforethought*, was published in 1931. His opening is one of the most famous in fiction:

❝ It was not until several weeks after he had decided to murder his wife that Dr Bickleigh took any active steps in the matter. ❞

Iles was one of the pseudonyms of Anthony Cox, writer of detective stories. Why his change of direction, then, when detective fiction was in its heyday? He explained it this way:

❝ The detective story is in the process of developing into the crime novel... holding its reader less by mathematical than by psychological ties. The puzzle element will remain but it will remain of character rather than a puzzle of time, place, motive and opportunity. ❞

It just took longer than he expected.

Celia Dale, *Sheep's Clothing*.
John Fowles, *The Collector*.
Graham Greene, *Brighton Rock*.
Patricia Highsmith, *Strangers on a Train*.
Reginald Hill, *The Spy's Wife*.
Francis Iles, *Malice Aforethought*.

Ira Levin, *A Kiss Before Dying.*
Daphne du Maurier, *Rebecca.*
Georges Simenon, *The Man Who Watched the Trains Go By.*
Barbara Vine, *A Dark Adapted Eye.*

Woman in jeopardy and romantic suspense

Suspense fiction is enjoyed equally by men and women readers, although the number of women writing it is higher. There are, though, two types of suspense novel which are particularly popular with women readers. They are known as woman in jeopardy novels (or woman in peril) and romantic suspense. They are both ultimately reassuring to the reader.

In woman in jeopardy novels a female protagonist is at risk and the story is about her struggles to overcome. Unlike many other heroines she has no special skills, physical strengths, influential friends or useful knowledge. The reader must feel she's ordinary, much like the reader herself. She's likeable; and she's also Sleeping Beauty, to be awakened not by a kiss but by the intervention of Life into her tedious world. Life means danger but she finds the resources within herself to rise to the occasion. The woman in jeopardy ends the book a stronger and wiser creature ready to play a full rôle in life, something she was ill-equipped for when the tale began.

Romantic suspense is a term more commonly used in the United States and it covers a hybrid born of a marriage between suspense and romantic fiction. The novels are lighter in tone than other suspense novels because of the prominence of the love story. They boil down to tales about a woman seeking love. Her quest may, for instance, uncover a plot against the lover who rejected her.

The intrigue may involve a crime but the pivot of the novel isn't an investigation of it. Instead, it's her attempt to resolve a situation in a way that enhances her emotional life. While the reader is enthralled by her adventures, the heroine is rapt in the mystery of her man's true nature. While she sets out hoping to win him, what she learns may encourage her to replace him with a preferable model or to take a break from entanglement with men. Publishers prefer these books to be the length of romantic novels, usually longer than crime.

Evelyn Anthony, *The Tamarind Seed.*
Mary Higgins Clark, *Where My Pretty One Sleeps.*
Robert Goddard, *Past Caring.*
Andrew Klavan, *Don't Say a Word.*
Susan Moody, *The Italian Garden.*
Mary Stewart, *My Brother Michael.*

Thrillers

Thrillers are usually treated separately from crime and suspense fiction because the demands on the writer are different. They are less introspective, less concerned with feelings than fisticuffs. But like many a crime novel, the thriller is a fast-paced adventure with plenty of physical activity and a terrific climax in the final pages. Thrillers are seldom written by women. Stakes are high in the world of the thriller hero. He needs to be tough, both mentally and physically, because he's up against incredible odds and, typically, the safety of countries and continents rests in his hands.

Raymond Chandler summed them up thus.

> ❦ The thriller is an extension of the fairy tale. It is melodrama so embellished as to create the illusion that the story being told, however unlikely, could be true. ❦

Three versions dominate: international thriller, spy thriller and political thriller. Each has its special emphasis. The international thriller is a big scale production, with the action taking place in several countries and revolving around crime. Wartime exploits could be included in this category, too. Typically there's a quest plus a determination for justice or revenge.

The spy thriller is about treachery and the reasons for it rather than about crime. The reader enters a precarious world of half-truths and convoluted plots but isn't required to deduce anything, as in the detective story, only to have faith in the hero who will save the day or wreak vengeance as appropriate. Often stories hinge on the uncovering of a plot against the state or, perhaps, betrayal of the intelligence community. They tend to be introspective rather than action-packed, and are rated the most intellectually demanding of thrillers. Among the best are Graham Greene's *The Human Factor.* Other espionage thrillers might be pacier, with the heroes as knights errant tearing their way through simple plots peppered with scenes of sex and violence.

Spy stories of both types enjoyed a vogue during the years of the Cold War but their popularity nose-dived after the collapse of Communism in Eastern Europe. Interestingly, spy fiction was a peculiarly British invention and failed to attract American writers, with the exception of Charles McCarry who wrote about the world of US intelligence. When I interviewed McCarry for *The Guardian*, on publication of *The Miernik Dossier*, his first novel featuring the spy Paul Christopher, he reluctantly revealed his own career as a CIA agent.

Political thrillers rejoice in the Machiavellian pursuits of politicians. Michael Dobbs's *House of Cards*, about a Member of Parliament who lets nothing, even murder, stand in the way of his ambition, was a spectacular success when adapted for television. Heavy on intrigue and treachery, political thrillers may skip crime entirely.

Sometimes the word thriller is used as a catch-all for every kind of fiction that promises the reader a prickle of apprehension and a lively yarn. Crime, suspense, ghost stories and horror stories are suddenly all encompassed. But the thriller is actually distinct from these other books, and thriller writers regard themselves as a separate breed. Their aims are different and so is the way they work.

A man who identifies himself today as a thriller writer is declaring that he isn't primarily interested in detection or charting subtle shifts in human relationships. But while his books may appear to be all 'up and at 'em' scraps between good and evil, they rest on a raft of painstakingly gathered facts. As much research may go into the making of a thriller as into a non-fiction book. They are enjoyed by readers who like learning about places, business, politics, past events or historical periods in an entertaining way, without recourse to non-fiction. And these readers will end up thoroughly well informed, because modern thriller writers vie with each other about the extent of their research.

Equally important, though, is the skilful way they apply it to determine their stories. Frederick Forsyth's novels are outstanding examples. For his first, *The Day of the Jackal*, he took an actual moment in French history and imagined a plot to assassinate President de Gaulle then. Truth underlying fictional events lent the narrative authority.

If you want to write a thriller, a background in Interpol or espionage may give you a headstart, but don't spurn your experience in other fields. Most of us know *all* we know about horse racing from reading Dick Francis.

It's no surprise that thriller writers say a novel begins with fascination with a subject, and the story evolves afterwards. The novel must make full use of setting and subject. Whereas other writers might legitimately blur a detail of which they aren't sure, it's incumbent on the thriller writer to get it right. The readers demand it, and anyway a thriller writer has the cast of mind that insists on doing so.

Robert Louis Stevenson wrote an excellent thriller when he penned *Treasure Island*, arguably the first of them. The basic ingredients remain the same today. Agreed Jim Hawkins is hardly a tough guy, but he's a courageous hero who captures the reader's sympathy. The cast is virtually all male, goodies are pitched against baddies, there's chicanery, greed, ferocious fighting, and a striking villain in Long John Silver. And, oh, the setting! Pirate ships and an island in the Caribbean.

In the last quarter of this century the thriller has proved one of the most commercially successful forms of the novel. It has attracted many authors who are good at cranking up the tension from page to page, by dint of short sentences in plain words; and a few who use the English language as elegantly as John le Carré.

Eric Ambler, *The Mask of Dimitrios.*
John le Carré, *The Spy Who Came In From the Cold.*
Len Deighton, *A Small Town in Germany.*
Michael Dobbs, *House of Cards.*
Frederick Forsyth, *The Day of the Jackal.*
Graham Greene, *The Human Factor.*
Adam Hall, *The Quiller Memorandum.*
Robert Littell, *An Agent in Place.*
Alastair Maclean, *The Guns of Navarone.*
Charles McCarry, *The Miernik Dossier.*
Robert Louis Stevenson, *Treasure Island.*

— Feminists and other axe grinders —

The peril of polemic is that you ruin a potentially good novel by lecturing the reader. If you are writing because there's something you are keen to say, that's excellent. But a novel allows you scope for considerable subtlety and there's no need for you to write a tract or to oblige your characters to harangue each other. No, you can get your points across more effectively than that.

It's a bit cheeky of me to single out feminist writers, when they have done so much to invigorate the genre, but some of them do provide a convenient example of what can go wrong when an author has 'a message'. Successful feminist writers are producing fine novels that show strong-minded modern women working as detectives or active in other kinds of crime or suspense novel. The stories might concentrate on an aspect of women's lives, such as late motherhood; but whether they do or not, they are implicitly commenting on our society and women's status in it.

Unfortunately, less capable writers fear that isn't enough and go for overkill. This approach resulted in the notorious scene where a woman who discovers a corpse during one detective story delivers a feminist speech before troubling to scream or report the matter. Need I say the drama vanished? The pace flagged? Worse, the reader giggled?

The lesson wasn't lost. One of the ways in which women writers discuss feminist novels among themselves now is to ask: 'Is it messagey?' The way to avoid being 'messagey' is this. Decide what your message is and then weave a story around it. However serious the statement you wish to make, your first duty to the reader is to entertain. He opens a novel because he fancies being told a story, not clouted with statistics.

When I wrote *Curse the Darkness*, during the property boom of the eighties, I was angered by the widening gulf between rich and poor. In the area where I live unemployed people had begun sleeping on the streets and the house next to mine was being squatted, while at the same time young home-owning couples were inheriting parental houses and turning into millionaires.

I made up a story about an impoverished literary novelist called John Gower who schemes to become famous and therefore rich. He fakes his disappearance but, when a boy is found dead near his hideout, he panics and flees. Unable to raise cash or support from his agent, he moves into a squat. Meanwhile, a parallel story featured Rain Morgan, my journalist heroine of several novels, investigating the murder of a once-famous screen writer.

The stories converged, and by the end I had touched on all the things I wanted the book to say about that selfish, uncaring decade. But there wasn't a slogan in sight. My story had put the argument for me, by illustrating the increasing difficulties under which some people struggled to survive and the ease with which others, including Rain and her friends, had a damned good time.

I have quoted a social and political example rather than a feminist one to emphasise that *any* message about which you feel passionate can put your novel at risk. Another example, then. Those using the genre to write about ecological issues are almost routinely heavy-handed, presumably because they are juggling the science of their subject and the art of fiction. When it comes off, a novel that shares important information with the reader as well as giving him memorable characters and a gripping story is extremely satisfying for both reader and writer.

Lesley Grant-Adamson, *Curse the Darkness*.
Val McDermid, *Kick Back*.
Joan Smith, *Why Aren't They Screaming?*

—— Working on your novel 3 ——

Categories

1 Into which category of crime or suspense fiction does your story fit? Remember that I have offered rough guidelines and there are no precise formulae.

- Modern whodunit: private detective or amateur sleuth?
- Modern crime novel?
- Police procedural?
- Historical detective?
- Hardboiled detective?
- Noir: very hardboiled?
- Comic detective?
- Thriller? International, espionage or political?
- Suspense?
- Woman in jeopardy?
- Romantic suspense?

Setting

1 Write down the sort of place you have chosen for your setting and any special circumstances. Not just an English village but *an English moorland village cut off in winter*. Not a mere island but *a private island during the hurricane season*. Or a factory *after the strike*. Or West London *on carnival weekend*.

2 Note any apt phrases you have thought up to describe its appearance or atmosphere. It would be a pity to forget them and leave them out of the novel.

3 Local traditions or events could make colourful scenes in your novel. Record any that you know of. Perhaps the island is famous for pearl fishing; or the ancient craft of thatching has been revived in the region where your village lies.

4 Write a few paragraphs to capture the way the setting looks in your mind.

5 Can you answer these questions about the setting?

- Which season is it? Unless it's a world unto itself, like a submarine, the time of year matters.
- What is the weather like? How does this affect the sea, the sky, the scents in the garden and the feel of the wind?
- What houses or other buildings are you going to use most often? Your hero's flat? The killer's manor house? The odd job man's caravan? Describe them, too.
- Make sketch maps of the district showing where the key buildings and landmarks are situated in relation to each other.
- Sketch the front elevation of any buildings, to help you remember whether they are double-fronted or single, have front gardens or open on to the street etc.

Or:

Work on story or character if you haven't done so yet. See exercises at the ends of Chapters One and Two.

4

PLOTS AND PLANS

I don't plan, you know; I start a book and wait to see what happens – to see if I can entertain myself. If I don't want to know what happens, sure as hell nobody else is going to. If I don't want to read it, I don't want to write it. Eric Ambler

It's a curious fact that if you take a roomful of crime writers and ask them the difference between story and plot, an embarrassingly high number will mutter that they really aren't sure. At first this seems absurd, as they are plotters *par excellence*. While an ordinary novel need not have a plot, a crime novel always does. Therein, of course, lies the answer. For crime writers, making up a story *is* plotting. They are doing what comes naturally and to ask them to specify stops them dead.

A handy way of illustrating the difference between story and plot is to quote what E.M. Forster wrote, in *Aspects of the Novel*.

❦ We have defined a story as a narrative of events arranged in their time-sequence. A plot is also a narrative of events, the emphasis falling on causality. "The king died and then the queen died," is a story. "The king died, and then the queen died of grief," is a plot. The time-sequence is preserved, but the sense of causality overshadows it. Or again: "The queen died, no one knew why, until it was discovered that it was through grief at the death of the king." This is a plot with a mystery in it, a form capable of high development... a plot demands intelligence and memory also. ❦

That pins it down very neatly, and Forster brings us mystery if not yet crime. How would it be if the person who 'discovered' the reason for the queen's death was lying? He might have been covering up the fact that she was killed to prevent her becoming regent until her son could succeed to the throne. Perhaps an inquisitive page boy plays detective. Or perhaps it's a crime novel centring on the murderer, his motives and remorse.

Take a hard look at the notes for your own novel and ask yourself what the plot is. Perhaps you have already written your story down in the form of a plot. Otherwise this is a good time to do so. A paragraph will be enough, as you needn't go into detail unless you prefer to. Take Forster's second example as a model, if you like, and check that your plot résumé encapsulates the mystery.

There is a dual purpose to this exercise: to help you understand how your story operates, but also to persuade you that you probably had a plot all along and needn't have been fretting that creating one was a task demanding mental gymnastics beyond the average brain. We are all natural storytellers and instinctive plotters, too. Because you are focusing on a crime or suspense novel, it would be very odd if you haven't been quietly plotting away, albeit unaware. Now that you have clarified your plot at its simplest level, you may feel ready to consider plotting your novel, which is to say shaping the story to make the most of the plot. But wait. There are a couple of other things to think about first, because the way you plot will depend on what you decide to do about them.

Writing is such a personal activity that there's no correct line of progress from here to the finished novel, but what I am going to alert you to in this chapter are decisions best taken before you begin to write. By leaping in without making conscious decisions on these points, you will take *un*conscious ones; and although you will be capable of setting down words on paper, you will run into trouble before long because the book wasn't thought through. Briefly, the things to decide are: at which point to start the story; from which viewpoint to tell it; and how to break the narrative into chapters.

Viewpoint

Viewpoint and starting point can make the difference between a successful novel and one that misses the mark. Let's consider viewpoint first. We touched on it in Chapter Two because I was anxious to warn beginners about being over-ambitious and trying to handle the viewpoints of more than one character in a first novel. Novels are more likely to fail because they are too complicated than because they are direct. Unless it's essential for your story to cut between modern characters and others living through earlier events, you have a choice in the telling of the tale.

Your decision about viewpoint will depend to a large extent on your central character. A vigorous, alert, reflective and sensitive fellow will make it easy for you to tell the tale from his angle. But a shy, bedridden and bored character will make it tough. There is no difficulty in writing boringly, but it's hard to write entertainingly about boredom.

Let's suppose you are planning to tell the story from the point of view of your central character. When you plot the novel in detail you will have to ensure he's on the spot for important events. If he missed the scene where the gang planned the bank raid, then you won't be free to write it. Instead you may have one of the other characters tell him about it later, which of course will lack immediacy and be less vivid.

How to cheat

In principal, the author of a single viewpoint novel isn't allowed to cheat by sloping off to share other viewpoints when deemed convenient. However, in practice, an occasional sloping off serves very well, providing it's brief. You can do it like this. Say there's a scene with your detective hero and one of the suspects in the case. The detective encounters the neighbour while she's gardening and they stand on her path and talk. All this is written from the detective's point of view.

The reader learns that his impression is that she's a sweet old thing upset by the tragedy, and guilelessly telling him the truth. But as the interview ends and he walks down the path you can linger on her, and you can let the reader see what he misses: the woman's face twisting into spitefulness and her secateurs reaching out and savaging the rose bush. In a sentence, you have added a dimension to the scene, by revealing the woman's personality and the detective's inadequate understanding.

These ploys are especially effective at the ends of chapters when you want to hand the reader a little surprise to egg them on. Providing they are kept extremely short, no one notices that you have slipped out of the bonds of the single viewpoint narrative. But when they are of any length, and frequent, they become distracting.

Two or more viewpoints

If you plan to juggle two or more viewpoints, you would be wise to fix a policy for chopping between them. Are you going to share the chapters out in order, like a card player dealing a deck? Or will you slide from one character to the next during chapters? Is the novel going to be arranged in groups of chapters devoted to each viewpoint?

In the last method they are usually called Book One, Book Two, and so on. Dividing the text into Books is a method reserved for long and complicated novels, usually when the action takes place over a long period of time or among different sets of people. Writers who succeed with them have a flair for organising their material and dovetailing the stories in the separate books.

But with any kind of multi-viewpoint, you are building in extra technical challenges. Be prepared for fancy footwork about timing, for instance. Cutting from one perspective to another can involve doubling back over the happenings of, say, Tuesday afternoon. You also have to be vigilant about balancing the attention each character gets from the reader.

It's more common for men to tell stories from the viewpoint of male characters, and women from the viewpoint of females, but there are plenty of examples of authors crossing over. We need look no further than Patricia Highsmith who was repeatedly drawn to write about pairs of male friends, quite apart from her outstanding series about Tom Ripley.

Writers generally regard crossing over as an additional challenge but for you it may not exist. I have been well on the way to a first draft before noticing that a novel of mine lacks leading female characters. (*A Life of Adventure.*) The more introspective a novel, the greater the risk of blundering. Recognising this, I made certain my second drafts were read by men primed to cry foul when my fictional men behaved and spoke like fictional women. I also obliged American friends to check that Jim Rush, the hero of that novel, was acceptably American.

There's a hackneyed piece of advice that writers should write about only what they know, but life would be extraordinarily dull if we stuck to that and so would our books. Be more adventurous by all means, but be prepared to submit what you write to the opinion of someone who genuinely knows the country, the profession or trade, as you do not.

Person

And then there's the matter of which 'person' you are going to use. Is your story to be related by one of the characters saying 'I', in which case it will be the first person? Or is the narrator an authorial voice saying: 'They did this and they did that', in which case it will be the third person? It isn't impossible to use the second person, 'you', but it's rare. (Jay McInerney did in *Bright Lights, Big City*.)

First person narratives often appeal to beginners because writing one feels like being an actor and slipping into disguise. Actually, a novel could be made up of more than one character addressing the reader in the first person, but to attempt such things you require a good ear for voices because each of them must be instantly recognisable.

American writers are notably fond of 'voice' novels in which their characters speak to the reader direct, and their private detectives continue to copy the lively speech of Chandler's Philip Marlowe. In Britain, detective novels are as likely to be in the third person as in the first.

Starting point

Once you have decided which character's viewpoint you are going to use, and whether it's to be a first or third person narrative, the next question is where to begin the story. The type of novel you are planning will influence this. At one end of the spectrum we have the detective novel with the linear structure. Stories, which is to say the detective's case, begin at the beginning; the investigation is followed through its middle period when suspects are checked out and the background of the dead person is fully examined; and the story arrives at the end, with the murderer apprehended or at least named.

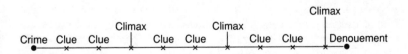

The traditional linear detective story

Novels about private investigators repeatedly open with new clients walking into their offices and hiring them. You may argue that an opening scene that has two people sitting opposite each other in an office is a pretty drab affair, despite the fact that they are discussing murder (which they are probably not doing in Britain given that private detectives aren't in the business of catching killers). No matter, this is a traditional opening which keeps the structure neatly linear and no readers have ever protested at it. They know the form when they approach a detective novel. Thrills are guaranteed later and they are happy to go through the minuet that proceeds them.

Flashbacks and fancy footwork

Other crime novels aren't necessarily linear and may be sophisticated pieces of storytelling using technical tricks such as flashbacks, unless they open near the beginning. You may start one of these at any stage of the story, with any kind of scene you choose. Take this example. You have a story about a young woman leaving New York for her childhood home in Russia where she solves a family mystery. You may choose to begin the narrative as she arrives in Russia, rather than when she was in New York months earlier forming the plan to go there. Or you may dive into it at a still later point, perhaps during the scene in the Russian town when she realises that the matter her family was oh, so coy about was, in reality, a crime.

Students tend to fret that their stories will turn out too short unless they start at an early point, but this isn't a serious factor because, as the narrative moves along, background to the action can be filled in and so the early material is not discarded. Perhaps the woman in Russia receives a phone call or a postcard from her husband or friend in new York. It causes her to reflect on her relationship with him, on her exile, and on the tussle she went through before booking her flight. As you see, no material has been lost but it has been repositioned and made less prominent.

Thrillers, detective stories and various kinds of crime novel are structured around characters going out and about, having adventures and making discoveries. Although the books might open fairly quietly, they erupt into startling adventures. By contrast, the typical suspense novel draws in on itself instead of expanding. Tension builds as the characters' suffering increases. They are like moths circling the lamp that singes them. Before long, nothing else exists for them except their suffering.

Whereas the detective novel has a linear structure, suspense novels have been depicted as spirals: in the early chapters they describe a small world which gradually gets smaller and smaller until the climax. This method of writing suspense develops tremendous intensity, for the reader is as tightly focused on the problems as the character who is suffering. (Daphne du Maurier's *Rebecca*.) All of this suggests that the favourite starting point for this kind of suspense novel is at the quiet beginning, but this isn't so. You may begin anywhere, as long as you keep tightening the tension, closing the circle.

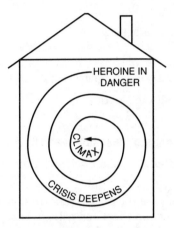

The suspense novel is a spiral

I believe that in crime and suspense novels it's usually desirable to introduce the protagonist at the outset and involve the reader with him quickly. You may have excellent reasons for doing otherwise. Perhaps you are writing a thriller and want it to burst on to the page with a description of a car blowing up. Or you want to use the scene where an imposter creeps to a patient's bedside disguised as a nurse and administers the fatal dose. Don't, though, leave your hero on the sidelines for long because the reader may become confused about the nature of the story and on which character he's intended to focus.

Plotting

Once you have chosen your viewpoint, decided whether to use first or third person, and settled on a starting point, you are ready to embark on plotting the novel. Writers develop individual ways of doing this so I will describe some common ones.

For this one you will need a list of the main events in your story. At the top you write a word or two to describe the episode you have decided should be the starting point of your narrative. In the Russian story I used as an example, the note would be something like:

J. arrives in Leningrad and meets P.

Or, if you are starting later:

J. discovers a diary in the *dacha*.

Below, you list all the other main events, insofar as you know them, in the order in which you currently think they should appear in the book. The final point in your list will be what happens at the end of the novel. For the Russian example it might be:

J. challenges P. with the truth.

Or:

P. persuades J. to keep the family's secret.

This is only a list of salient points, you aren't concerned with chapters yet.

The points in the list are the bricks with which you will construct the novel. Run your eye down them and notice where the various characters come into play. It's foolhardy to thrust lots of characters at the reader in the first few pages, better to introduce a few and gain his confidence in you as a writer before you gradually add the others. Equally, it isn't good to put off for many chapters the arrival of significant characters.

Late on the scene

Crime writers, though, face a peculiar problem and this may be something you need to address now. The modern crime novel, when it isn't simply an updated version of the classic detective story with a linear structure, may require the late arrival of significant characters in the shape of Detective Inspector Wizard and his colleagues. Indeed, the good inspector will inevitably influence the way the story develops. Your villain runs from him? Engages in a battle of wits with him? Dupes him? Regardless that yours is the type of story where the police are ultimately foiled, their intervention will have a profound effect.

There's no smart side-stepping of the problem of bringing in these important figures in the final chapters, just an acceptance that crime writers have a dispensation to do so. It isn't elegant but it is necessary. Should you wish, you can devise ways of sneaking references to them into the story earlier, but even so they won't have a real presence until their hour comes. Policemen don't.

Looking down the list you will probably spot things you want to swap around. Supposing you bring forward the introduction of the hero's colleagues, then that makes nonsense of the sequence as it stands. Perhaps you have realised it would make easier reading if the neighbours, who feature in the sub-plot about marijuana in the greenhouse, were held back until the reader has become familiar with the ménage of the international drug dealer who has bought the old manor house in the village. Take a pencil and number the points in a fresh running order. Erase and rewrite until you feel you have achieved the most entertaining result.

This may be laborious, because every change you make will suggest others, but it's time well spent. Also, when your story involves puzzle-solving, a list enables you to position the clues at good intervals and to see at a glance where they are.

Alternatively, some writers prefer to jot the key points on slips of paper and shuffle them around on a table until they achieve the greatest effect. After that they list them or mark them on a chart to pin on

	Mary	Celia	Dennis	Rufus
6.55	At home alone	Walking home	At station	In car alone near wood
7.10	At home with Dennis	Finds body in wood	At home with Mary	In car alone
7.20	At home alone	Tries broken call box, then runs to pub	Walking to pub	In pub
7.25	At home alone	In pub	In pub	In pub

Chart showing characters' movements at crucial times

the wall by their desks. Writers who specialise in detective stories find that making a chart, showing who was where and when, helps their plotting. They can be reminded at a glance who had a swiftly confirmed alibi and who can remain under suspicion for longer.

--------------- **Chapter plan** ---------------

Once you have finished plotting, you can turn your mind to a Chapter Plan. This is the magic tool that helps you manage your material and keeps you on track once you begin to write. Again, writers have evolved various ways of doing it and I shall offer a couple you might like to try.

The first depends on that list of points. Write it out again but in the running order you have chosen. Then draw a pencil line through it where you think the first chapter should end. This may encompass several points, such as your heroine's arrival on a Caribbean island, the strange absence of her host and the drunken intrusion of a neighbour. Then draw a line to separate the events you want to go in the final chapter. Perhaps that involves the host's shame-faced return after a sojourn in a prison cell, and your heroine's success in proving the drunken neighbour was murdered by drug runners. Divide up the rest of the points in the same way.

There is no ideal number of chapters that you ought to aim for and length varies from short ones, say 2,500 to 3,500 words, to long ones, perhaps 10,000 words. Long chapters are usually broken up into segments with white space between them. Whichever length you expect to write, bear it in mind when chopping your list into chapters.

The marked list is an embryo Chapter Plan. To make a fuller one you will need more sheets of paper, one for each chapter. Better still is to use a notebook with facing pages. On one page write out what you want to go in chapter one. Keep it in the form of a list but expand the information. (Later you will keep notes about chapter one on the facing page.) Work your way through your chapters until you have a full Chapter Plan. When doubtful about anything, put a question mark beside it to remind yourself that it may not be the best solution to the situation. When you have finished making the plan, read it through and you should get the impression of reading a telegrammatic version of a novel. *Your* novel.

Research

A word about research before you are tempted to disappear into the fictional world of your chapter one. Research is much talked about, and especially by people who don't write novels or aren't efficient at researching for them. Too often research is an excuse for delaying writing or working on the preparation of a novel.

This is how police record fingerprints

Now that you have your Chapter Plan you will have a fair idea what sort of thing you need to find out. If it involves police work, then the public relations department of your regional police headquarters will have the answers. When you approach experts, in any field, be specific about what you want to know. People are usually friendly to writers and keen for us to get things right. Whenever you are doubtful about where to get information, ask at your local library. Possibly the library will stock books on the subject, or you may be handed a reference book listing organisations you could approach.

We all go through life with a jumble of misinformation in our heads so don't be reluctant to confirm things you think you already know. You could prevent yourself basing your whole novel on a misconception, as one author did when she wrote about a Devon family falling on hard times because the man was imprisoned for failing to meet his gambling debts. Gambling debts aren't enforceable at law.

And then there's the kind of research you do when you walk around with a notebook, struggling to capture the essence of a place. I learned a vital lesson about this when I wrote my first novel. It opens with Rain Morgan arriving on holiday in a village, one where my husband and I had owned a cottage for years. Had I set the story in high summer, it would have been full of mistakes. Because we let the cottage for holidays, I didn't see the place in summer until the year after the book was published. The seasonal change astonished me.

I learned never to trust film or television, books or old photographs, let alone visits at the wrong season. Vegetation changes, views are opened up or hidden as trees blossom or lose leaves, quiet places become crowded and vice versa. Besides, the length of the day will influence your story. When I began *Patterns in the Dust* with the line 'October was dying', I was signalling dark evenings when comings and goings might not be observed and a young woman who didn't reach home before nightfall could find herself terrifyingly trapped.

The purpose of research

The purpose of research is to underpin your story with truth. It isn't to boast how many books you have read, countries you have trailed around or experts you have consulted. Ideally, in the finished novel your slog should be all but invisible. After all, if the reader wishes to read a textbook or a travel guide, then he can do so as easily as you did.

What the good researcher does is learn enough about his subject to avoid making errors. Writing about a character who is a dry cleaner, you will want to be sure that when he makes a passing reference to a chemical he's referring to one which dry cleaners actually use. But you won't, I trust, be tempted to recite us his process for removing the egg stain from your tie plus a breakdown of the chemicals he would use to do it. Yes, it sounds laughable when the example is a high street affair such as dry cleaning, but we have all picked up novels which bow beneath the burden of technical detail.

Researching for a novel can be curiously serendipitous. Information bobs towards you on the tide of events, and you have only to recognise how you can use it. You choose to set your novel in a little-known part of Spain, and when you open your newspaper there's an article on it. You are toying with writing about a mystery in the art world, and suddenly there's a television programme about missing Old Masters.

Sometimes the convergence of fact and fiction can be alarming. When that happens you have to decide how to react. In January 1994 I began writing *Wish You Were Here*, a novel about a man who lures and kills women. The setting I chose was Gloucester, a city I lived in during the Sixties but hadn't previously used in fiction. In March the newspapers were suddenly full of the horrific discoveries at 25 Cromwell Street. I had to choose whether to resite my novel in another town or to keep it in Gloucester and refer to the police investigations. I chose the latter. Only the opening scenes are in Gloucester, but 25 Cromwell Street casts a shadow over the rest. I used it as a motif.

How do you know when you have done enough research? You don't and when you are part way through your novel you will realise that more information is needed. You can't tell this in advance. Characters may reveal hobbies you didn't know they had, and you have to pick up a book on the rules of real tennis. Or a city whizzkid is rewarded with a fantastic new car and you have to trot along to a car showroom. Or the hero takes his wife away for the weekend in Wales, to a place you picked because it was a comfortable weekending distance from his base, but now you need to see whether it looks as pretty in reality as it does on the map.

Some writers take a break during their first draft and do the extra research; others prefer to push on to the end of the first draft and catch up on it then. Whichever way you do it, keep a record of the points of which you are unsure. The page facing the Chapter Plan is a good place to do this, because you will know where the information is to be slotted into the text.

Violence

Skimming over your Chapter Plan, you may have qualms about the level of violence. Depending on your personal taste, it may strike you as either too violent or not nearly violent enough. This is an issue that exercises the minds of crime writers, and where two or three are gathered together lively debates ensue.

Violence is subject to fashion, on the page as well as on the screen. After the savage seventies came the slightly gentler eighties, but they were followed by the nauseating nineties. The novelist and critic, Julian Symons, writing in the updated *Bloody Murder* in 1994, regretted the emphasis on violence (high body counts; sado-masochism) in current American fiction. With typical asperity he complained of some much vaunted exponents:

> ❛ Line by line and page by page they are extremely bad writers, their only virtue energy. ❜

Their prose is hacked about as badly as their victims, and the result is closer to the horror comic strip than the novel. In the wake of the Rosemary West murder trail, with its evidence of what the forensic psychologist Paul Britton labelled predatory sadistic sexual psychopaths, it's impossible to use the argument: 'Such things don't happen here'.

Laura Cummings, reviewing for *the Guardian* the work of an English follower of the fashion, objected that there's no suspense in the current crop of ultra violent books. 'Muscles without tension,' she called them, regretting the authors' failure to aim higher than cataloguing brutal acts.

Interviewing British crime writers, I discovered that most set themselves standards. A commonly adopted guideline is that the reader shouldn't be handed information that could result in a copycat crime. So, if the recipe for a bomb is required by the plot, crucial details will be omitted. In my *Curse the Darkness* a murder is disguised as a hanging, and although I researched how it can be done I didn't publish the information. One of the other self-imposed rules many writers adhere to is that the victims shouldn't be children. They reject the subject as too distasteful for them to work on; and they have no wish to titillate the susceptible reader.

Male and female novelists writing comparable novels take a similar attitude to violence, although it has to be said that males are more likely to choose the types of novel that allow more scope for it. Detective story writers may skirt around it, except for describing the finding of the body, because their hero arrives after the slaughter. Stories told from the killer's viewpoint can hardly dodge it, though.

In the end, it isn't the number of bodies or the subject matter that makes the difference between a novel which is widely admired and one that readers can't stomach. Anyone can write a bloody scene, describing the flying gouts of blood and the crunching of bones, but it takes talent to make it an effective piece of prose. Which may be a way of saying that art can get away with anything.

Working on your novel 4

Perception and perspective

1 From whose viewpoint are you going to tell the story?
2 Which voice will you use? First person (I) or third person (he, she, they)?
3 What is the starting point for the story?

Plotting

1 Write down the main events in the story as you fancy telling it.
2 Notice where the main characters come in. Are you leaving your hero in the wings for too long?
3 Take care that you don't burden the reader with too many characters in the first pages.
4 Do you need to rearrange events to make the story more suspenseful or exciting?

Chapter Plan

1 Once you are happy with the plot, make your Chapter Plan.
- Draw up a fresh list of the *main* events in the order in which you have settled they should appear.
- With a pencil, mark off the points you want to cover in the first chapter. Remember that chapters can be anything from 2,500 words.
- Do the same for the final chapter.
- Then do the chapters in between.
- Devote a whole page of a large notebook to each chapter, and list *all* the points you want to mention when you start writing. Leave the facing pages blank for comments and reminders which can then be written directly opposite the points to which they refer.

Reading list

Anton Chekhov, *The Shooting Party.*
Henry James, *The Other House.*
Joseph Skvorecky, *The Sins of Father Knox.*
Elleston Trevor, *Bury Him Among Kings.*
Margaret Yorke, *No Medals for the Major.*
Oscar Wilde, *The Picture of Dorian Gray.*

5
WRITING THE FIRST CHAPTER

Writing is only applied linguistics and Shelley was wrong, we're not the unacknowledged legislators of mankind.   Angela Carter

Writing a novel requires a judicious mix of imaginative flair and meticulous organisation. One won't succeed without the other. Organisation comes so naturally to some writers that they are hardly aware they are doing it, but the rest of us need to evolve ways of keeping on the chosen path. The Chapter Plan is the most valuable tool for doing so. Once you have written your plan and done your preliminary research, you are ready to begin writing. In Chapter Seven I discuss the equipment novelists use, but for now I want you to consider the creative act of writing rather than the mechanical. Here you are, then, ready to write *Chapter One* on the first page of text.

Gather together any notes, maps or other documents that have a bearing on this chapter and clip them together. While you are writing you can refer to them swiftly instead of having to hunt them down and lose your momentum. It's tiresome to have to rewrite a scene or make other changes because you failed to remember correctly.

First scene

No doubt you have been thinking for some time about your first scene, although you may have done so only when choosing a starting point for the novel and perhaps the scene isn't worked out in detail. Either way, this is the moment when you pose tough questions about it.

Your potential reader would judge the book by its first page, and you want to make sure he would decide to buy rather than put it back on the shelf. You judge books that way yourself, and you know how quickly one assesses them. In spite of a snappy title, an eye-catching cover and a blurb peppered with words like 'pacy', 'chiller', 'haunting' and all the rest used to promote crime and suspense fiction, if the first page doesn't hold your attention, you aren't inclined to read further.

This isn't to say every story must explode on to the page with a gun-fight or similar drama, but it ought to start off in, more or less, the tone in which it means to go on. For instance, characters who are to be thoroughly frightened as a suspense novel develops could be made uneasy by an incident in the first scene, and the reader given a fore-taste of what is in store for them.

But suppose an author begins a serious thriller with a comic incident. This hardly hints at a book that is thrilling or haunting. Indeed it suggests the opposite. And although by page three the lighthearted atmosphere may have given way to tension, how is your reader to know? An ideal first page sets the tone and tempo you have chosen for your novel. Action-packed, anxious or ironical, the first paragraphs are a trail-blazer for the rest.

Tone

If you are in doubt about the tone of your novel, ask this: 'What feeling does my story arouse in *me*?' Fear, perhaps? Whatever the answer, your task during the thousands of words to come is to create the same emotion in the reader. This isn't nearly as difficult as it sounds because when you write a passage that makes you excited or anxious, it's likely to do the same to anyone who reads it. The occasions when you want the reader to feel most strongly are at the climax at the end, and at other climaxes during the story if the book has these. Of course, a novel contains its lighter moments as well as its darker ones, but it's the overall impression you are concerned with here.

Pace

The days when the first scene of a novel was a preamble about characters and places are long gone. Now we like to have something going on straight away. An accomplished first scene contains the seeds of the story to come, reflects the atmosphere of the novel, introduces at least one important character and enough mystery to entice the reader to turn over to page two, and from page two to the end of the chapter. There's no leeway for padding or waffling in your first chapter. That is where you establish the pace of your story, a pace you must maintain to the finish.

As the author, you may find it hard to gauge whether you have achieved that crucial page-turning quality because you will become over-familiar with the first scene. Posing the following questions helps. Have you, in the first 300 words (which is roughly the number that appears on the first page of a published text), hinted at the conflict which is to form the basis of your story? Have you alerted the reader that this is a tale of danger, suspense, double-dealing or what you will? Is the setting indicated? And is your imagery appropriate to the theme of the book as well as to the scene?

When you are satisfied on those points, consider this one. How does your first page look? A slab of solid text? Two or three paragraphs of equal length? You can improve on this by breaking up the grey wodge of type into paragraphs of varying lengths. A brief, crisp opening sentence is an excellent idea. Many writers favour chopping up the text on the first page into paragraphs that range from one line to no more than four, arguing that this is easiest to read and creates a sense or urgency.

I say it all depends on the individual novel and what tempo and tone you wish to achieve. A scene presented in staccato fashion may not be in tune with the rest of the book. You, as a reader, are well qualified to judge whether you admire the short and sharp look and wish to adopt it.

Opening paragraphs

Memorable first paragraphs (sometimes called introductions or intros) are apposite. They give a clear idea of your subject and the tone in which you intend to tell the tale. If you can think up a beautifully rhythmic sentence, so much the better.

Daphne du Maurier's *Rebecca* begins with the natural, flowing line:

❝ Last night I dreamt I went to Manderly again. ❞

It's so right for the book that it's astonishing to learn she almost preferred something else. However, there's encouragement to be drawn from her hesitation. As the famous first line was an afterthought, it may not be imperative that you delay writing *your* first scene until you have perfected the opening line.

Nothing hooks a reader faster than a touch of mystery. Look again at the famous beginning of Francis Iles's novel *Malice Aforethought*, which I quoted in Chapter Three. It contains the shocking revelation that Dr Bickleigh has decided to kill his wife and raises questions about the steps he took and the reason he delayed. From his first lines the wily author has you fascinated to know *what happened next*. And this is the nub of suspense fiction: you grab the reader and don't set him free until you have finished. You keep titillating his curiosity, with surprises and mysteries. He can't get away because he needs to know *what happened next*.

Here's a selection of introductions from a variety of novels that come to hand, some modern and some not. First, Georges Simenon and *The Hatter's Ghosts*, an unforgettably atmospheric suspense novel first published in 1949.

❦ It was the third of December and still raining. The figure 3 stood out, huge, very black, with a sort of gross belly, on the stark white of the calendar, set to the right of the till, against the dark oak partition separating the shop from the shop window. It was exactly twenty days ago, for it had happened on the 13th of November – another squat 3 on the calendar – that the first old woman had been murdered, near Saint Saviour's church, a few steps from the canal. ❦

As you know, Simenon was a Belgian who wrote in French. This is a translation by Nigel Ryan. Simenon was always at pains to use plain language. You see how potent it is in this excerpt: no fancy phrases to hamper the reader, just a strong visual image in sombre colours of an ordinary subject, but followed by the shock of multiple murder. In those three sentences he conveys the brooding tone of the story to come.

By contrast, Margaret Millar in her introduction to *The Soft Talkers*, a suspense novel published in 1957, gives us the chief characters, plus dialogue that encapsulates the mystery.

❦ The last time his wife saw Ron Galloway was on a Saturday evening in the middle of April.

"He seemed in good spirits," Esther Galloway said later. "Almost as if he was up to something, planning something. More than just a fishing trip to the lodge, I mean. He's never really enjoyed fishing, he has a morbid fear of water." **9**

In *The Talented Mr Ripley*, published in 1956, Patricia Highsmith immediately creates the edgy feeling that pervades the book.

6 Tom glanced behind him and saw the man coming out of the Green Cage, heading his way. Tom walked faster. There was no doubt that the man was after him. Tom had noticed him five minutes ago, eyeing him carefully from a table, as if he weren't quite sure, but almost. He had looked sure enough for Tom to down his drink in a hurry, pay and get out. **9**

Len Deighton pitches straight into dialogue in these first lines of his spy novel *Berlin Game*, published in 1984 during the Cold War years. The exchange juxtaposes the personal and political, as the book does.

6" How long have we been sitting here?" I said. I picked up the field glasses and studied the bored young American soldier in his glass-sided box.

"Nearly a quarter of a century," said Werner Volkmann. His arms were resting on the steering wheel and his head was slumped on them. "That GI wasn't even born when we first sat here waiting for the dogs to bark." **9**

Sue Grafton, the creator of Kinsey Millhone who solves the 'alphabet murders' in Los Angeles, begins *C is for Corpse* with a brisk six lines in the voice of her hardboiled heroine. The book was published in 1986.

6 I met Bobby Callahan on Monday of that week. By Thursday, he was dead. He was convinced someone was trying to kill him and it turned out to be true, but none of us figured it out in time to save him. I've never worked for a dead man before and I hope I won't have to do it again. This report is for him, for whatever it's worth. **9**

P.D. James startles us with the corpse and the central mystery in *Unnatural Causes*, which came out in 1967. Her beautiful prose is always a counterpoint to the horrors of which she writes. The description of the mutilated corpse in the boat takes up six paragraphs of roughly similar length, indeed the whole of the short first chapter, so I shall quote only the first paragraph. Superintendent Adam Dalgleish doesn't appear until the second chapter, but by that book he was a well-established series hero.

❦ The corpse without hands lay in the bottom of a small sailing dinghy drifting just within sight of the Suffolk coast. It was the body of a middle-aged man, a dapper little cadaver, its shroud a dark pin-striped suit which fitted the narrow body as elegantly in death as it had in life. The hand-made shoes still gleamed except for some scuffing of the toe caps, the silk tie was knotted under the prominent Adam's apple. He had dressed with careful orthodoxy for the town, this hapless voyager, nor for this lonely sea; nor for this death.❧

Finally, a daring opening to Ruth Rendell's suspense novel, *A Judgement in Stone.* In one line she gives away the name of the killer, the names of the victims and the killer's motive. And in the next few she reveals the result of the crime.

❦ Eunice Parchman killed the Coverdale family because she could not read or write.

There was no real motive and no premeditation; no money was gained and no security. As a result of her crime, Eunice Parchman's disability was made known not to a mere family or handful of villagers but to the whole country. She accomplished nothing by it but disaster for herself, and all along, somewhere in her strange mind, she knew she would accomplish nothing. And yet, although her companion and partner was mad, Eunice was not. She had the awful practical sanity of the atavistic ape disguised as twentieth-century woman. ❧

You may have your own favourites which you can also study to discover what lures you to read on. Once you have identified what you want to achieve in your first lines, try writing them. You might be lucky and get it right at once, but you are more likely to want to polish and improve. Keep all your attempts in case you decide to reconsider. And don't fear that you must perfect your first lines before moving on to write the rest of the scene.

Style

Style is another of those words that make novice writers nervous. How do you acquire a good writing style, and is it the same thing as a writer's 'voice'? The essence of good style is that the language flows, words are used correctly, the rules of English grammar aren't flouted, and the reader finds it easy to follow the narrative.

For some time there has been a vogue for writers of literary novels to adopt an artificial style, far removed from the way in which people speak. No harm in that, but it would be an impediment were you to write your crime or suspense novel in that way. Complicated syntax, elaborate imagery, arcane vocabulary, and comparable showing off by the author, make it virtually impossible to produce a story with the pace readers expect in this genre.

Writers in every language and every age have offered us their definitions of good style. Seneca believed:

> ❛ Style has no fixed laws; it is changed by the usage of the people, never the same for any length of time. ❜

Aristotle's view was:

> ❛ Correct idiom is the foundation of good style. ❜

Skipping to this century, we find Evelyn Waugh proposing three aims for writers: lucidity, which you can acquire; elegance, which you can strive for; and a distinctive voice, for which you can only pray.

Cyril Connolly's discussion of style, in *Enemies of Promise* which was published in 1938, is still worth reading. Briefly, he was writing at a time of change in authors' attitudes to style and he didn't approve of the shift. Until then they had made a distinction between the language as they spoke it and the formal, carefully structured English they wrote. When a few authors, including E.M. Forster, broke the convention and decided to write novels in the direct language of everyday speech, there was controversy. Critics complained that as writing became plainer it was converging with journalism. They feared that literary style would cease to be valued for itself, and that we could reach the point where the best style was deemed to be one of which the reader was unaware.

Well, those things came to pass. The style which doesn't impinge is admired as 'transparent'. In fast-paced genre fiction it's an asset because we want nothing to delay the reader on his dash through the story. Indeed an author may take a deliberate decision to strip his language of complexities and literary flourishes in favour of whizzing the reader along.

Another author (and in this group I include myself and all those who have come to fiction after decades of disciplined writing for newspapers) may find that 'natural' is what comes naturally. Highsmith and Simenon are two who preferred the unadorned style. It has, I believe, a hidden advantage: its simplicity runs counter to the trickiness of the plot and, in this way, it subtly misleads the reader.

Good style continues to be subject to fashion. Adjectives used to be heaped one upon another to give the reader a picture of the scene as the writer envisioned it. Now it's considered better to limit oneself to the occasional well-chosen adjective. Well-chosen may mean either the correct word used precisely or an unexpected word that achieves a striking effect by offering a fresh perspective.

Adverbs were once notoriously over-used and now they are sparse. It's no longer acceptable to employ them to describe the manner in which each action is performed. 'Languidly' or 'hurriedly', perhaps. Neither are they tacked on to every line of speech to emphasise meaning. There never was much point in: *'Oh, I don't know,' she said doubtfully,'*; or *'Yes, I will definitely come,' he said positively.'* You can encourage a good style by reading your work aloud, listening for clumsy sentences and repetitions of words and phrases. Ears pick up blunders that eyes miss.

When is a cliché a cliché, and do they matter? Clichés are useful bits of shorthand. (*Cold as the grave*; or *Shaking like a leaf.*) They are apt descriptions that have been over-used. Therefore they are regarded as poor style and a lazy way of writing. Weed them out of your text where possible.

Writing in *The Guardian*, the novelist Sebastian Faulks made this amusing observation about lazy language.

❦ "Unfailing" is an adjective that took secret marital vows to the noun 'courtesy' in the register of popular English usage. Their brief ceremony followed that of "staunch" to "Conservative" and "dire" to "straits". The couple are now seldom seen without each other in public. ❧

You can collect your own happily marrieds and vow to divorce them.

Sloppy use of language can shake the foundations of your story. One of the words whose meaning is being corrupted by misuse in everyday speech is *alibi*. People have begun to treat it as a synonym for *excuse*, but it isn't one. When a suspect tells your hero that he has an alibi he must mean that he was somewhere else at the time. The word doesn't mean anything other than that. Another legal term under attack is *sub judice*. That means that a matter is before the courts and, generally, can't be written about without risking prejudicing the impending court case. Sometimes councillors who don't want to answer questions announce that a matter is *sub judice*, although what they mean is that the council itself is going to look into the problem. Or a businessman will cry *sub judice* because an internal enquiry is going on at the factory. You and your sleuth should bear in mind that it isn't a shield to protect those with something to hide. At least, not until they have gone to law.

Voice

Your voice is the rhythm of your prose, the kind of thing you say and the way you say it, the length and construction of your sentences, and the vocabulary you automatically reach for. It doesn't vary significantly whether you are writing a novel or a letter to a friend. Although you may need to strive to achieve good style, in the sense of clear language that says what you want it to say and avoids grammatical mistakes, your voice is already present. Providing you aren't trying to ape another writer, what you set down on the page will be in your own voice.

David Lodge, the novelist and critic, had this to say about voice when he spoke, in 1995, at a Royal Society of Literature symposium on the teaching of writing:

> ❛ There's a chemical reaction between form and content. Even a single sentence in a novel is the result of cause and effect that reaches deep into the author's psyche. ❜

Dialogue

Dialogue serves several purposes in a novel. It conveys information, reveals character, and it relieves pages of grey text. Writers often get carried away with dialogue, because it's fun to do and once two or three characters are chatting you can be reluctant to shut them up. Also, if you are among those writers who tot up pages as you go along, you will discover you have hit upon an easy way of filling space. Yes, dialogue needs to be tamed. Every exchange should move the story forward, either the main strand or the sub plot, and if it helps both of them so much the better.

Is slang OK? Sure, provided you reckon your readers will cotton on. Context may help them if the words are unfamiliar. Myself, I am wary of slang because I grew up in two different areas of the UK and discovered, through many a gaffe, that slang meant one thing in one place and the opposite in another. Later I could sympathise with the friend who shocked colleagues by saying her husband was 'on the randy'. Where she came from it meant he was having a social evening with friends. For her listeners 'randy' had a strictly sexual meaning.

Recently, in a detective story set in Wales (David Williams's *Last Seen Breathing*), I spotted 'grafter' being used to describe a person who always wants something for nothing. In various corners of England I have known it to mean a hard worker. And so on. When the gap is as wide as the Atlantic, the scope for cultural misunderstanding is vast.

But there's another reason for considering how much modern vernacular English your novel should include. Well-written crime and suspense fiction can stay in print for a long time, longer than most other genres and literary novels, but with outdated language this is less likely. Dame Ngaio Marsh, extremely popular in her day, has survived despite all colloquialisms, but read one of her books before you make your decision. If you find it muddling when, for instance, an 'old man' turns out to be a small boy, you might get a taste of how today's common speech will seem in years to come.

It's good to talk

In a novel involving detection or a quest of another kind, your hero might have a companion with whom to share ideas about the mystery. Their dialogue can enhance the novel, providing you keep the byplay in check. True, these exchanges allow you to reveal their relationship – pointing out, for instance, which is the witty one and who has the sharpest perceptions – but you must resist becoming bogged down in the fun they are having together.

Their conversations are your chance to recapitulate and suggest interpretations of events to date, but also to move the story forward as they consider possible future developments and plan their own actions. But when all they have done is argue about who let the kettle boil dry, or who can make the sickliest sandwich, then they have done nothing to maintain the pace of the story.

Writers with a good ear for dialogue are blessed indeed. They can produce conversation that seems absolutely natural, and the speech of their characters is differentiated, preventing confusion about who is speaking. This is a skill all novelists can hone but it helps to be sure what you want to achieve. I referred just now to speech that 'seems' absolutely natural, and that's a precise description. If it were truly written in the way we speak to each other it would be dreadful because we are too often ungrammatical, repetitious and longwinded; or else we interrupt when we anticipate how sentences will end, and we break off our own sentences when we are interrupted.

Colloquial or literary?

Fiction isn't the art of copying down real life, and one of the decisions facing you is whether to make your dialogue colloquial or literary. There are degrees, of course. Should you take the literary option, and allow your characters to construct and deliver sentences in decent English, you aren't banned from letting them lapse into the spluttering vernacular at moments of stress. To do so is a device for reflecting increased tension. And the exacting standards you set for your main characters needn't apply to all. The most eloquent of heroes may find himself in conversation with someone whose first language is slang or who has a hazy grasp of syntax.

One reason writers choose colloquial speech is that they feel this makes their books easier to adapt into television scripts. Ready-scripted dialogue might make a book an attractive proposition, but writers who produce novels with an eye to adaptation have a shrewd idea of television's other demands, and tailor their work accordingly. The depth and detail of a well-crafted novel may not be required. As Elmore Leonard, who has written his share of Hollywood scripts as well as novels, said in an interview for *The Times*:

> ❛ When you reduce a novel to a screenplay you lose most of the good stuff. All you have left is the plot. ❜

In the same breath as slang comes dialect. Dialect is seldom used these days, partly because it's an impediment to the reader but also because we are more sensitive to the feelings of those who dislike being guyed. It's tricky to write without patronising the speaker. You can just about get away with it in small snatches, and preferably in a comic situation. In my first book I used a very little West Somerset dialect, for local colour and in the mouths of a group of villagers in the pub. I can't say how well its purpose was understood once it was translated into Japanese.

Good dialogue is whatever is appropriate to your book and your characters. The following remark comes from Easy Rawlins, the Los Angeles hero of Walter Mosley's noir novels.

> ❻ Everybody was peeing on my head. And telling me it was rain. ❾

For contrast, this was the reply of Adam Dalgleish, P.D. James's hero, when someone in *Unnatural Causes* suggests he's often asked why he chose to be a detective:

> ❻ Not many whom I care to answer... I like the job; it's one I can do reasonably well; it allows me to indulge a curiosity about people and, for most of the time, anyway, I am not bored by it. ❾

Because they favour 'voice' novels, American writers take a different attitude to dialogue. For them it is less a tool for imparting information than a chance to reinforce character by replicating the speech patterns of the types of people in their pages. That sounds freer than it is, as though they take it straight off the street and shovel it into their books. Not so. American dialogue is no more natural than any other, just tailored differently. For a master class read George V. Higgins.

Indicating speech

There are a variety of ways of indicating speech and thought on the page. You have to choose and then be consistent. We no longer write '*he said*' before or after each line of dialogue, but we often follow it with a sentence explaining what the character thought or did as he spoke. Who hasn't had the experience of reading a series of exchanges and losing track of who is saying what?

Brilliant writers of dialogue may feel this doesn't apply to them, but for the rest of us it's a sensible precaution to limit to three or four the number of lines spoken before characters are identified again. You may do it by putting in the occasional '*said Peter*' after he has spoken. Or you may preface his next remark with:

Peter snapped back at him: 'What makes you think I was there?'

Computer typesetting saw the introduction of new type faces and these have had an influence on the appearance of the printed pages. Double quotation marks seldom enclose lines of speech now; we have learned to use single quotes instead. A journalistic habit of preceding speech with a colon instead of a comma has crept across to book publishing.

He said: 'Listen...'

You might also notice a European habit of omitting quotation marks altogether and indicating speech with a dash at the beginning of the line.

– Look out, we're going to crash!
She shielded her face with her hands.

Indicating thought can be done as baldly as writing:

He thought about the ...

or it can be done by switching from ordinary (roman) type to italics:

'Are you sure you want to do that?' *Oh God, don't let her do it. Please God, don't let her.*

Your choice will depend on whether you intend to use italics for anything else, such as flashbacks. On the whole, readers don't care for pages of italic print and flashbacks are better indicated by leaving white space on the page before and after the flashback sequence. Where the sequence is very long, then it could form a separate chapter.

The size of it

As I mentioned earlier, chapters don't have to be of equal length. It is far better to write as much as you need and not a word more, than to pad out a chapter to a particular length. On the other hand, if you have a chapter that's a lot longer than you planned you might want to think about making it two. Usually a chapter ends when a scene does but some authors are prone to break during a scene, regarding this as a trick to lure the reader into the next chapter.

How long should your book be? The more traditional the detective story, the shorter; and the shortest length is 60,000 words. Anything less and a publisher will be alarmed at the prospect of a novella, always the most awkward length to market. But check in the book shops for the number of pages in new novels of the kind you are writing (not reprints of earlier titles) and you will be able to gauge the publishers' current requirements.

At the time I am writing this, suspense novels and modern detective novels are expected to be about 75,000 words, and thrillers perhaps ten thousand more. But these figures fluctuate and you will wish to be up to date.

Clues

As you write from scene to scene, the true nature of your characters has to be revealed gradually. You strip away the layers of their personalities, and thus they develop into interesting and complex individuals. At the dénouement, no one will be dissatisfied. Not only have all the clues pointed to that conclusion but so have the characters' moral weaknesses. You will discover as you go along that you are learning more about them and you may wish to pause to reassess, particularly if you were unclear about the theme when you began.

Your insight into human nature will guide you during the writing but, when tackling a detective story, you must also be deft at placing clues. Writers who excel at clues include Colin Dexter, who relishes devising them. Your clues to the killer's identity should be plentiful but may be tucked away in a paragraph that tells the reader about something else of, apparently, greater significance. This way you play fair and provide the information but the reader is gulled into missing it.

Another trick is to heighten the drama immediately after planting the clue; the change of pace forces the reader to go scooting by instead of pondering the lines that contain the clue. This principle of revealing information while slyly distracting attention from it applies to most novels within the crime and suspense genre.

Working on your novel 5

Writing the first chapter

Time to begin writing your first chapter. If you are planning fairly short chapters you might like to finish it. When you break off writing, read through and check the following points.

- Do your first few paragraphs catch the tone of the novel?
- Is there a hint of the story's conflict or mystery in them?
- If something exciting is happening in the chapter, is the language active or passive?
- Have you made the setting clear?
- Are the paragraphs of varying lengths, especially on what would become the first page of printed text?
- Have you used dialogue to enliven scenes?
- Does your dialogue convey information about the story as well as about the personality of the speakers?

If you have to answer 'No', then repair the faults.

Or:

If you don't know what your first scene is to be, you can do the same exercise with another key scene further on in the chapter plan. Writers often write one or two scenes out of sequence when they get a flash of inspiration and want to set something down quickly,

Reading list

Cyril Connolly, *Enemies of Promise.*
Len Deighton, *Berlin Game.*
Sue Grafton, *C is for Corpse.*
George V. Higgins, *Trust.*
Patricia Highsmith, *The Talented Mr Ripley.*
P.D. James, *Unnatural Causes.*
Ngaio Marsh, *Artists in Crime.*
Margaret Millar, *The Soft Talkers.*
Walter Mosley, *Red Death.*
Ruth Rendell, *A Judgement in Stone.*
George Simenon, *The Hatter's Ghosts.*
David Williams, *Last Seen Breathing.*

6

SUITS WRITER ...

To live in the word of creation – to get into it and stay in it – to frequent it and haunt it – to think intensely and fruitfully – to woo combinations and inspirations into being by a depth and continuity of attention and meditation – this is the only thing.

Henry James

If this is your first attempt at a lengthy piece of fiction you will also have been discovering your physical needs as a writer. Perhaps you set out thinking that a corner of your bedroom would be an excellent place for your desk and chair, but were bothered by traffic noise and had to make your camp elsewhere. Or you were lucky enough to have a whole room set aside for writing, only to find you were entranced by the garden, the flying clouds and marauding cats, and had to swing the desk around to face a blank wall. Far better a blank wall and the pictures in your head than any other entertainment.

The romantic notion of the writer is a solitary struggling with the muse in a country cottage. The owner of a remote house in Wales used to advertise it to let: *beautiful landscape, miles from the road, spring water, no electricity, suit writer.* Well, not this one. It might be fine for a Celtic saint but we writers are preoccupied folk without time to struggle up a mountainside to check whether a sheep has died in our water supply. The disappointing truth is that you can fall prey to distractions anywhere. Isolation and dramatic scenery won't immunise you.

Without going to the romantic extreme, there's much to be said for temporarily dodging the pressures of your everyday life, either while a first draft is hammered out or perhaps while you rethink and polish a later one. Richer novelists are known to hole up in hotels, while others

retreat to country cottages where they can concentrate without benefit of family and friends. Most though, have to learn to ignore the
ringing of the doorbell, unplug the telephone and use psychological
tricks to create an inviolable space for writing. When working at
home is genuinely impossible, then the reading room of the public
library may prove your haven.

A very small number of writers rent offices and go out to work set
hours each day, because this is what suits them and, it follows, what
they can afford. They are chiefly men and like to consider their work
a business. Naturally, we almost all aim to make our living by our
writing but the majority see themselves in the world of art and craft
rather than business. The question is one of philosophy rather than
writing.

———— Occupational hazards ————

However you organise it, being a writer involves spending an inordi-
nately long time sitting down, fingers tapping and, especially when
using a computer, head held virtually still. Comfort is crucial. Writers
are prone to suffer backache and neck problems, and also risk repetitive strain injuries.

A chair that causes backache is a health hazard. Try out every one in
the house to find which you can use without discomfort. There's no
edict that insists you perch on the same one all day. Most computers
can be raised on a box or books to get the screen to the required
height, although laptop models can't be adjusted. If you find you have
to jut your chin or sag your spine to read the screen, you have got it
wrong. A few hours of hunching and jutting can give you a nasty crick
in the neck, plus pain in your shoulders and lower back.

Repetitive strain injury is disabling. Sufferers endure considerable
pain and their hands become unable to function. Sadly, since the
switch from typewriters to computers the condition is no longer rare
among writers. You can be a victim at any age. The most popular the-
ory to explain the recent susceptibility of writers relates to the differences between typewriters and computer keyboards.

Manufacturers of computer keyboards have opted for the same style
of flat plastic box with slightly dished keys packed close together.
Gone are the days when every few minutes we pulled out a sheet of

paper, set it aside, reached for another one, rolled it under the platten, straightened it, lowered the bar, and resumed typing, swinging the carriage at the end of each line. In other words, using a typewriter demanded a range of hand and arm movements, and we swivelled our heads and shifted the position of our bodies as we made them.

At the first suspicion that your hands feel sore or your wrists stiff, break off for a while and either rest them or do something completely different. Yes, I know you want to complete your novel but it isn't worth being crippled in the attempt. And remember, typing is a skill easily acquired. To be kind to your hands, make it a ten finger exercise instead of putting all the pressure on a few. You don't even need to attend classes. I learned from a borrowed book.

Make it your practice to take short breaks from your desk. Next time you're stuck for a phrase don't just sit there while you think, get up and wriggle your shoulders, stretch your hands, exercise your wrists and walk around the room. No need to take your mind off your hero's pithy riposte when he's charged with the murders he's investigating, but you do need to give your body a rest.

─────────── **Fully equipped** ───────────

Time was when readers and authors used to discuss books but these days the questions lobbed at writers are about the equipment they use. During the nineteen-eighties the debate was typewriter versus computer. Now computers are assumed. But, please, don't be deterred from writing because you don't have one. They are a useful tool but not essential. The important thing is your novel. By all means write it by hand or read it into a tape recorder. As long as the result is legible or audible, you can pay to have it typed later. Specialist typing services advertise in magazines for writers. By the time your novel reaches a publisher it must be cleanly typed, but what you do before then is up to you. More about publishers in Chapter Nine.

It's untrue that all the mystery of the writer's art is contained in grey plastic boxes. To know that I worked on the original portable (Osborne), which was succeeded by an Amstrad (PCW5812) and then by an Apple Macintosh (Performa 475) reveals nothing except that, until the most recent purchase, I spent as modestly as possible. I didn't necessarily use the software programmes that came with my cheapish boxes. A programme that took forever to scroll through a ten thousand word chapter, while I was creating a second draft, was sheer frustration so I bought a different one and was able to flit around the text instead. Although I didn't require anything fancy, I did demand flexibility and speed. And so will you.

When buying a computer, bear in mind that the salesman is unlikely to be a closet novelist. He probably won't grasp that a writer's requirements are limited to simple word processing by equipment that is as user friendly as the industry gets. He may not realise, or he may not tell you, that publishing and the media have adopted the Apple Macintosh. His job is to sell but yours is to choose.

In the mood

It took me far longer than it ought to have done to start writing this book. Lack of enthusiasm wasn't to blame, merely the feeling that I was over familiar with the subject and, as usual, my mind was teeming with fresh ideas I wanted to explore in fiction. I had prepared a detailed outline, I had signed a contract and agreed a delivery date; but I also had an intriguing idea for a new novel, editors were hoping for short stories from me, London was suffocating in a heatwave, and my comfy domestic life was disrupted by my cleaner resigning and my husband becoming editor of a London paper instead of working from home.

These excuses look pathetic now I've set them down, as feeble as writers' reasons for avoiding work normally seem to everyone else. There are, I'm afraid, endless reasons writers find it difficult to start or to keep at it once they have started, and it's as well to be prepared for this problem because you will certainly meet it. I'm not talking about writer's block, an altogether more daunting situation, which means a writer loses the instinct to write and can remain in limbo for months or years. Professional writers are justifiably nervous of it happening to them, but of the numerous novelists I know there's only one who has suffered writer's block. There's no cure. One waits for the day when one begins once more to feel and think like a writer. Here, though, I'm talking about the petty difficulties everyone has to overcome.

Nothing can be done about the serious things in life getting in your way. Bereavement, love affairs and births aren't intended to be ignored. But it *is* possible to shut out the inconsequential. Writers have to steel themselves to be selfish, and adopt self-defence tactics. Anybody who works from home is fair game for friends and family who fancy a chat. As a writer, let alone a novice working on a first novel, well, so much the worse: you're only sitting around making up stories, aren't you? Hide behind an answering machine and return calls at *your* convenience. Failing that, unplug the telephone.

Don't Want To days

But supposing there isn't anyone else to blame? Suppose you are simply not in the mood to write this morning? What then? We all have Don't Want To days but it's usually possible to turn them into productive and enjoyable days. All it takes is a little psychology. First of all, go to your writing room or to your desk, or if you work on the kitchen table then fetch your work and set it out as you normally do. In other words, pretend everything's going to be all right. Quite often it becomes all right as soon as you are in the room, at the desk, or have the paraphernalia of your work around you. You have entered your writing environment and your mind automatically engages with the story. This is one of the reasons it's valuable to have a special space for writing.

If things haven't come right by this stage, carry on pretending. Read over what you wrote the previous day. Ideas on the page will stir memories of what was to come next or they will spark off new lines of thought. Start writing. Maybe it's slow for the first paragraph or two, but no matter. You are writing and you have conquered your reluctance. For this day, anyway.

Writing a novel is demanding and lonely, a wretched way to pass time, you can think of any number of things you'd prefer to be doing, and you don't know why you aren't doing them. No doubt you'll think like this on dreary Don't Want To days. So why don't you do those other things instead? Because no one else will write your novel for you, that's why; and if you don't press on with it, neither will you.

A musician can persuade another player to take his place in the orchestra and can go to the beach. They can both play Mozart, and the audience won't mind which does it because the sound will be much the same, anyway. But your novel is special and there's no possibility of delegating. It's composed of your personal ideas and feelings, your particular skills and techniques, the strengths and weaknesses of your individual talent. It draws, albeit indirectly, on your own personality and experience. It's peculiar to you and it speaks with your unique voice. And that is why you want to do it, isn't it? Not, ultimately, to satisfy an editor or a market, or to impress anybody else, but to enjoy the achievement of artistic creation. On Don't Want To days read this section. On bad ones, read it twice.

Tricks and ploys

There are tricks you can perform to stave off reluctance and enhance your automatic willingness to write once you are at your desk. Some writers leave an unfinished sentence or scene when they break off work for the day, and thus they are able to plunge straight in next time. A remarkably effective ploy is to play the same piece of music each time you settle down at the desk. It works like magic, instantly switching you into writing mode.

When I delivered my third novel to my publisher I was asked how I managed to produce it so quickly, and was happy to reply: 'Gin and Vivaldi.' The gin was my reward at the end of the long day and I had played *The Four Seasons* over and over and over... Asked about my second book, the answer would have been Beethoven's Violin Concerto. I wrote a play to the accompaniment of Vaughan Williams' *The Lark Arising*. Select your music carefully. Vocals, I think, would be intrusive. You aren't going to listen to it and you are only going to play it softly, perhaps just loud enough to drown out traffic noise.

The sexy bits (or coitus interruptus)

Sometimes there's a certain scene that you shrink from writing, usually a sexy scene. You wouldn't think it to read their books but a surprising number of writers feel silly about writing sex scenes and put them off. In my first book I cheated. After mentioning that Rain Morgan and the young archeologist went into the bedroom, I started the following paragraph with: 'Later...'. Instead of filling in the details for themselves, as I had lazily hoped, readers did a double take and wondered whether lines were missing.

The trouble with ducking out of situations when you are a novelist is that you arrive at the same point in later books. You have only delayed, so you might as well work your way through the problem when you first meet it. In several of my subsequent novels I had to provide a little bit of sex, and I evolved the following method. Where the awkward scene begins I leave myself a note on the page, as simple as: (*Insert hotel bedroom scene here*). Then I take up the story after the scene I'm avoiding. Another day, probably when I have finished the first draft of the book, I will sit in a cafe, order a cup of coffee and take out my pen.

It sounds ridiculous, I know; to be writing in public a scene, or a series of them, that I cringe from tackling in private. But it works and for this reason: I feel silly with everyone watching me writing, but I'd feel so much sillier if they were watching me staring into space and *not* writing. Thus it gets done.

Notebooks

Writers are individualists when it comes to choosing notebooks and experience will teach you which sorts best suit your method of working. The basic requirements are one slim enough to slip into a pocket or handbag and carry wherever you go, and a bigger one for writing down everything from story ideas to reminders such as: 'Don't forget Blank Street is one way'. On occasions when your smallest notebook is too bulky to carry, a plain postcard serves the purpose admirably.

Spiral bound books, or else flat pads, seem to me ideal because you can tear out the pages without them collapsing. Part of the planning process is to rifle through your notebooks, spot that nice exchange of dialogue, tear out the page and put it in a paper clip with all the other things to use in the same chapter. Reminders and notes made over a period of months won't be overlooked. When it comes to writing, they may be discarded. But they won't have been forgotten.

—————— Changing your story ——————

I expect you have noticed by now that a good deal of discarding goes on during the process of writing. Ideas that seemed exactly right when you concocted your story can reveal themselves as frivolous, too pat, and insufficiently exciting. Better ones spring to mind. As you become familiar with your characters, your innate understanding of the way human beings react in a crisis, or the way types of personality interrelate, prompts you to make changes. A few might be major, such as reinventing a character; others might be minor adjustments, perhaps turning close sisters into resentful stepsisters.

Changes beget changes. As the relationship between a couple of characters becomes a different one, the way others respond to them will alter. Close sisters are treated alike but, once they turn into rival stepsisters, people favour one or the other. They might admire the dreamy Mary and dismiss Martha as a drudge; or they might approve of Martha's practical commonsense and be irritated by Mary's foolishness. What they can't do is feel the same about both girls.

This sounds as though each change, however slight, involves you in comprehensive rethinking before you can go on writing, but in practice it's seldom so. True, you will need to rectify earlier pages when you prepare your second draft, but there's no urgency because there may be further changes to come. No, you can carry straight on with your narrative because you will automatically recognise the effects of the changes, just as you automatically understood the necessity for them. After all, you have been researching human nature all your life.

Never fear that to alter your story or characters as you go along is a sign of failure. If writing is a voyage of discovery, it's important that you take account of the things you discover. Provided that you cling to the framework – the basic premise of the story, the tone you want your novel to have and the conclusion you want to reach – then the rest is detail.

As change follows upon change, you may be wringing your hands over your Chapter Plan. How can you write the scheduled scene with the bad-tempered woman sergeant in the police station, when you have already suspended her from duty on suspicion of giving a prisoner a black eye? You can't, of course. But you could write one about the collapse of the scheme to clear her name. Or you could decide to skip any mention of her as, the way it has turned out, she's irrelevant in the chapter. There's a little danger here, the danger of appearing to forget a character.

Readers appreciate that the more words a writer expends on a character, the more attention the reader must also give it. Once you have built up the crotchety police woman into a figure the reader has come to believe is a relatively important actor in your drama, it's a mistake to allow her to disappear into oblivion for the second half of the book. There are two courses open to you. Either you let her fade out of the story, in which case you should reduce the reader's expectations by trimming her rôle in the earlier chapters. Or you bring her back in a key scene or two later in the book but, during the time she's offstage, you drop occasional references to her so that she isn't entirely absent.

Keeping a record

How on earth, you may be wondering, can you cope with all this upheaval? Beginners often abandon novels because of the apparent hopelessness of keeping track of what has gone before. Every step off the narrow path of the Chapter Plan takes them further into the mire, and yet they realise they must make changes. The solution I'm going to offer you is one I devised when I began writing novels and it has since been adopted by established writers as well as students. No doubt they have all introduced refinements to suit themselves.

It's extremely simple. Besides having a Chapter Plan, which tells you what you *intend* to write, you keep a chapter by chapter Record of what you *actually* wrote. After finishing a chapter, read through it scene by scene. Make a list, line by line down the page of a big notebook, of each salient point so that you encapsulate the chapter: the characters in it, the setting and the gist of the action. By underlining proper names in a contrasting colour, they will stand out at a glance.

Armed with this Record you will have a speedy means of checking back on earlier work as the novel proceeds and remembering grows more difficult. You will avoid time-consuming mistakes (thinking Joanna was in the office with Alphonse the day the ransom demand was posted), and you will save yourself ploughing through a stack of papers (or doing tedious computer searches) to refresh your memory. Details won't be in your Record, but you will be reminded that it was in chapter five that the boat was grounded on the shore, and so you can quickly flick through chapter five to see what Lucinda was wearing as she waded ashore, or what the level of the tide was, or whether you have used up your prepared description of the sea sucking on the shore or can confidently drop it in now, in chapter twenty-three.

And if you suspect too long a time has passed since a particular character took a hand in events, you can swiftly skim the highlighted names to find out when he was last mentioned. As you are doing this you will probably spot a convenient place to slot in an extra reference to him when you come to prepare your second draft. Make a note of it beside the Record. Our memories are unreliable and it's more efficient to make notes immediately an idea occurs to you.

Maps and sketches

Sketches of key locations and interiors are a safeguard against mistakes and sometimes suggest plot developments. When you write that Fred escaped through the bathroom window at the rear of the manor house and ran to the village without meeting a soul, your reader might recall that Mrs Greenfinger's vegetable garden adjoined the path he took, and that Mr Snoop was prone to lurk by her hedge in the hope of glimpsing her frisky niece. A sketch map would remind you that Fred must detour to escape unseen.

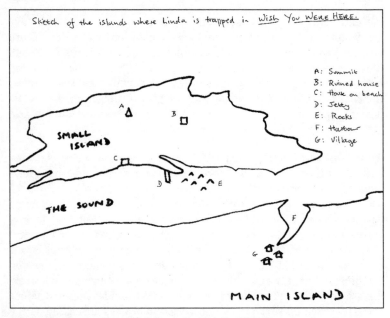

Sketch of the islands where Linda is trapped in *Wish You Were Here*.

Calmer scenes present pitfalls, too. When Mrs Scribbler settles down to write a letter, her desk had better be in the same room as the last time she used it or a lot of puzzled readers are going to wonder why. Mistaes of this nature aren't peculiar to the novice: a celebrated author of detective stories moved an important piece of furniture from one room to another without mention of removals men. But with a few sketches pinned to your wall and a Record at your elbow, you can skirt trouble.

Try not to be inflexible about the way you work. The perfect room, the irreplaceable pen, and the notebooks you particularly like aren't indispensable. And the day may come when you can't afford to go into a hotel to immerse yourself in your novel, you need to sell the cottage, and you are denied access to your study because your unfavourite cousin from Australia is sleeping on the floor. Well, there's still the public library.

——— Working on your novel 6 ———

1   Finish writing your first chapter. Make a Record of what you actually put in it. It will look something like this one, which I wrote for the second chapter of Evil Acts.

Chapter Two

Don Fricker visits *Grace* and asks where she heard noises.
She recalls visits with him when builders were working there.
Julian brings lots of possessions (his 'iceberg') to the house.
He hears night noises which she attributes to washing machine.
Petal hasn't returned again.
Noel, Liz and *Tess* come from Devon and can't find Bridge Street on the map.
Tess is worried about *Petal* being in London.
Julian drops in to pack for Edinburgh.
Mike Cleary calls with a ruse and then gets her to show him round.
He tells her the truth: he writes true crime and the house was *Jack Henrey's*.
Grace challenges *Fricker* about selling the house without telling her.
At the Dôme, then at her house, he talks to her about *Cleary* and *Henrey*.
She stays home from work yet another day.
She plans to sell.

---

2   Check these points:

- Have you invented details, incidents or minor characters as you went along?
- New information that couldn't have been in the Chapter Plan might call for subsequent changes. If you have invented an incident, say Adrian's arm is hurt in a scrap, you will want to remember it later. So, as chapter six calls for him to have a violent confrontation with Dave, you will be sending him into fray with a lame arm. On the empty page facing chapter six write yourself a reminder of the injury.
- Read aloud everything you have written and listen for clumsy phrasing, unspeakable dialogue and repetitions.
- Did your characters make sufficient impact when they were introduced?

Reading list

John Buchan, *The Thirty-nine Steps.*
Erskine Childers, *The Riddle of the Sands.*
Robert Harris, *Fatherland.*

Non-fiction

Julian Symons, *Bloody Murder.*

7

A GOOD IDEA
AT THE TIME

I've got to tell stories. It scintillates and shimmers in front of me, the whole idea of telling stories.   Elleston Trevor

There are rare geniuses like Simenon who produce excellent novels at a sprint, fifteen days in his case. By comparison most of us are plodders and we are inclined to grind to a halt here and there. I have already mentioned the Don't Want To days, when you look for excuses to avoid work, but there's another cause and, as a new writer, you may find your confidence severely dented when it happens to you, as it almost certainly will.

When it strikes you may be capable of continuing to put words on paper or you may abandon your desk in despair, but in any event you experience the sinking feeling that you have wasted your efforts. The project that seemed such a good idea when you were embarking on it is a flop. You don't seem to be getting anywhere. Or rather, where you are getting isn't where you intended to go.

The encouraging news is that virtually all writers are forced into these unplanned breaks and their work benefits from them. A number of writers tell me they slide to a halt a third of the way through each novel. Some get further in, and yet others find they break down two or three times before the end. The point is that we all have our own rhythms, and so will you.

Regard these pauses in your work as beneficial. It's as though there's a mechanism in a writer's brain that throws a switch when things are heading off in the wrong direction. No lights flash to tell you exactly what's going wrong, you have to work that out for yourself; but you are unable to enjoy writing until you have got to the bottom of the trouble. Invariably, a loss of enthusiasm for your work means something is awry.

When this happens, your subconscious is warning you it's time to stand back from your work for a few days, maybe weeks, and reappraise it. Leaving it untouched for a while allows your mind to disengage from it. Then you can come back to it refreshed and, if you are lucky, you may find that while you have been distracted by other things part of your mind has been unravelling the problem with the manuscript.

Quite possibly it will occur to you that the story is too thin and you would improve it by developing the sub plot; or by building up one of the characters; or by strengthening the plot with more twists and turns; or by dropping a character who hasn't entirely served the purpose you had in mind for her.

—————— Off at a tangent? ——————

Lacking a sudden revelation, approach the problem systematically. First, read your Chapter Plan and compare it with the Record to see where you veered from the outline. Check that you are happy that any changes you made were sensible ones. They probably were but there's a chance that you shot off at a tangent without realising that your new material was undermining your original story. If this is what has happened, you can either rethink the novel to follow the direction suggested by the new material, or else you can scrap what doesn't fit with your original idea and rewrite, following the plan more closely.

Unless you are very near the beginning of the book when you decide to rewrite, you may not wish to do it immediately. It may suit you better to list the changes you plan and then to press on with the first draft. Some people hate that sort of task hanging over them. Others prefer to see a pile of manuscript growing, regardless of the extent of the changes to be made later. Do whichever you are more comfortable with.

More research

Sometimes you may stall while writing because you reach a point where you need to do more research. This isn't always immediately apparent, and you may try to press on without realising why you aren't totally happy with what you are doing. Perhaps the additional research involves travelling and, as it hasn't been convenient for you to make the journey, you were putting it off until the end of the first draft.

More likely, new ideas have occurred to you in the course of writing and you need to get to grips with extra information. An interviewer who asked Elmore Leonard about writer's block got the reply:

❛ I don't believe in that. If I ever have a problem it will be with a character's background. Then it's a question of doing more research. ❜

Acting out of character?

Next, scrutinise your characters. One of the commonest mistakes in novel-making concerns the handling of characters. Work your way down your cast list asking yourself whether anyone is, literally, being made to 'act out of character'. In crime and suspense fiction, where plots are equally as important as personalities, it's crucial that your characters behave in a way that's credible, given what you have told the reader about them. Our stories are concerned with extreme situations and people pushed to the brink, but the moment a reader starts thinking: 'Oh, she wouldn't do *that!*' is the moment the spell is broken.

There must be enough in the character's personality, as you have described it, for it to be understandable that your heroine tackles the gunman herself rather than cringing in a corner over her mobile phone and dialling 999. Her courage or recklessness should be strongly suggested before that scene arises. Similarly, if your hero is to don a disguise and infiltrate a meeting of unscrupulous businessmen, readers should already be familiar with his cunning and his cool-headedness.

Characters can seize a writer's imagination and perhaps you find you have spent too much time with one when you ought to have been concentrating on the hero. It's ridiculously easy to slip into this and permit a character to overshadow the book. In this genre the effects are severe if the novel isn't tightly focused on the issues and the protagonist.

One reason writers fall into this error is that by the time they begin to write they are extremely familiar with their hero so, although he continues to develop on the page, the author's own interest may lie in the unveiling of lesser characters who weren't distinct when writing began. This may be the hero's girlfriend who takes to scene stealing. Or the hero may spend too much time fretting over her, thus keeping her at the forefront. The intention was for her to be important in his life but now she jostles with him for first place. A variation on this mistake is to give too much rein to minor characters.

I have described in interviews the pleasure of sitting down at the desk without knowing whom I shall meet that day. These little people, who hero and author encounter in their joint adventure, add sparkle to a novel but their contribution has to be controlled. It would be folly to meander off into their adventures and tilt the focus of the story towards them.

Often they are a means of injecting a dash of humour into a dark tale. They can be comical and amuse the other characters, or perhaps amuse only the reader as it isn't appropriate to give characters in a crime or suspense novel too many laughs. Used sparingly, these minor characters provide a light counterpoint to the main drift of the story. When they aren't comic, they may be striking in other ways. In fact, they are your chance to employ splendid characters who would be disastrous as protagonists because their quirkiness would weary reader and writer alike if too much was heard of them. Kept in their place, they are small treasures.

Remedies

When the wrong character overshadows, or the requirements of the plot force someone to act out of character, you have two options. You change the character or you change the story. Changing the story doesn't necessarily mean relinquishing scenes and incidents you have reason to be pleased with, but it might mean allotting them to a different character. That can be the neatest solution when people are acting out of character. Yet if your problem is that the wrong person has become dominant, the obvious answer – trimming – is probably the best one. However, before committing yourself to any reworking, consider all the possible changes you might undertake and select the one you believe will give you the strongest book.

With luck, you may not get completely stuck or disenchanted before realising you have hit a problem. Maybe you only have a vague feeling that something is unsatisfactory. In this case, give yourself time to discover precisely what it is rather than pushing on and hoping for the best.

Prose dull?

But what if you are happy about your characters and story, yet a niggling dissatisfaction persists? Perhaps it's the prose that's letting you down. Does your novel seem flat, the writing tired when it ought to be energetic? If you are able to read supposedly exciting scenes without stirring a flicker of excitement within yourself, they need improving. Does the tone of the writing seem flippant? Many writers aim for that, as a way of taking the edge off their unpleasant subject matter, but perhaps you didn't mean to and it happened because the humour got out of hand. That is easily put right.

Polishing is a task that can be safely left until later, after the first draft. Although you ought to jot down a reminder of the way in which scenes disappoint you, along with any ideas for improving them, I wouldn't urge you to rewrite them immediately. When you return to them later, once the first draft is completed, you will see them afresh and may take a different view from the one you hold now.

Being too familiar with scenes, and working them over and over, can result in dead writing. The fizz of crime and suspense fiction is largely achieved by your urgency to set down a thrilling scene. By all means correct and titivate later but don't sacrifice the invaluable effect of your initial enthusiasm.

Characters vague?

Another snag concerning your characters might be emerging. They are behaving in an entirely appropriate manner, but they don't have as much impact as when you created them. Go back to your original notes on them and see whether you have skipped over personality traits that might bring them alive, or have left out information about the way they relate to the other characters.

All this appears to be in order? Then how about the manner in which you introduced them? That entrance is their big moment, the one when they make an impression on the reader or fail to. Have you made the most of it? Look through two or three novels of the same type as yours, ones that you are familiar with and admire, and check how other authors do it. A useful trick or two might be borrowed.

Incidentally, if you are writing a detective story be wary of seeking tips from a book that isn't the first of its series. The series author faces the special burden of introducing her hero, plus his colleagues and lovers, time after time and has to cast around for new ways of doing it. But as you are working on your first novel, and there are no fans clamouring for the latest instalment, your needs are more straightforward.

Making an introduction

This is how Andrew Taylor introduced a minor character, the book shop owner, in his suspense novel *The Barred Window*.

> ❛ At the opening party there was orange squash for the children and sherry for the grown-ups. Aunt Ada shepherded Esmond and me towards our host, Mr Sandwell. Ignoring Esmond, he shook my hand and asked with an air of desperation whether I liked reading. He was a skinny man with a nose like a bird's beak and semi-circular ears set at right angles to his skull. When he talked, his fingers fluttered in the air at about the level of his thighs as though he were caressing the heads of pets which no one else could see.
>
> "Yes", I said, "I like reading."
>
> "Good, good. Splendid. Now where's Stephen, I wonder?"

Mr Sandwell floated off, his hands stroking and scratching the heads of invisible dogs. For a moment I watched him. He was moving steadily away from Stephen, not towards him. ❥

The man's anxieties, and that image of the invisible pets, pop into the reader's mind whenever Mr Sandwell is referred to from then on. And we have also learned that Thomas, the narrator, is a keen observer.

But in fast-paced stories you may prefer not to slow the action when a character is introduced. This is how Jim Rush meets the press photographer in my *Dangerous Games*. During the novel the man becomes a nuisance whom Jim can't shake off, a relationship signalled by their first encounter. As it takes place in the dark, there's scarcely any physical description.

❧ He rocketed out of his hiding place, slammed into the gunman sending him flying, recovered his own balance and was poised for renewed assault when his brain unscrambled words from the confusion and he hesitated.

"Don't shoot!" he heard. "Please don't shoot. I wasn't doing anything. You've got to believe me. Don't shoot."

The voice was English, southern, a soft country drawl. Terror raised it way above its normal level.

He peered down at the pleading man, said quietly: "I don't have a gun. Where's yours?"

He stood back and let the Englishman rise. The man was trembling, gabbling.

"Mine?" The voice was a squeak. "Don't be bloody daft."

He cut him off. "If neither of us fired that shot, then the guy who did is still around. I think he was on the road."

"Who are you?"

"What?"

"I'm Martin Peters. Who are you?"

"Jim Rush. Look..." He wanted escape, not acquaintance. He didn't conceal his impatience.

Peters said: "I mean are you the police?"

"Police?" An ironic laugh.

"I thought maybe..." He'd guessed wrong but he didn't sound altogether disappointed. "You're American, right?"

Jim cut in again. "That guy could be on his way round here right now. I'm not hanging about to check it out, OK?"

He dashed towards the trees, aware that Peters was sticking close. Jim planned to streak away from him once they reached a path. He was younger and fitter, especially now that Peters was winded from the fight. But Peters said he knew where the path was and once they were on it he kept pace and he kept talking. **9**

The scene is also the one in which Jim Rush, who featured in an earlier novel, is reintroduced to the reader. Up to that point the 'he' in the narrative is unidentified.

———— Theme uncertain? ————

Instead of character, story and prose, it may be theme that's bothering you. Assuming you are one of those writers who is unsure of the theme when you start, you might by this stage have a fair idea what it is and need to stop and reflect on it. Not only might changes be required to the early chapters to accommodate your theme, but you will inevitably want to point it up in the rest of the story which is as yet unwritten.

Time spent reflecting on the theme and the best means of illustrating it is always time well spent. Although you may be tempted to dash headlong through the story, content to know at last what your theme is, the result will be hit and miss. Some scenes, perhaps major ones, might not be in tune with it or might even be contrary. The effect can be confusing for the reader as you are giving out conflicting messages. This is a confusion easily avoided because, once you have identified your theme, relatively minor adjustments can pull everything into line.

On the tortuous journey through a novel, things change. Even if you were certain what your theme was when you began writing, you may grow uneasy about the way it's working out as chapter succeeds chapter. Time to break off and ponder.

This is how I coped when I realised that my third novel, *Guilty Knowledge*, was not proceeding exactly as I expected. The very first thing I had known about the book was that it was to be about loyalty, but this proved less precise than I supposed. As the work grew I became puzzled and had to pause to consider what was actually happening in the book. I see that in my notebook I headed a page *Themes and Moral Issues* and then wrote this summary.

'It is about the way people fool themselves into accepting the unacceptable. They do it because of greed although they fool themselves it is loyalty. The greed is in some cases for money and in others for prestige. Oliver taking advantage of Rain is a tiny example. Josceline's death provides an opportunity for them all to rethink their moral position *vis a vis* the deception. Only Barbara Woods is ready to do that and she is prevented, although she is *too easily* prevented. There is no strong moral will, no drive for the truth, and this diminishes them as people as well as artists.'

I had intended to write a book that looked askance at what I have always considered a questionable virtue, because of the way people use it as an excuse for behaving badly, but in the event I was tougher. The result was a superior book to the one I embarked upon.

For your eyes only?

You are still unsure where your novel is going adrift but what more can you do? Should you, for instance, ask someone else's opinion? This is one of those entirely personal matters. After a friend revealed he had glanced through my notes for a novel, it was impossible for me to work on it for days. He was genuinely interested in the craft of novelmaking, and I'm used to teaching and talking about it, which makes it sound a ridiculous over-reaction. But if you are susceptible in that way yourself, you will understand what an appalling thing he did. So, you have to decide for yourself whether you can bear anyone else's eyes on your work before it's completed.

The crime writer Joan Smith says that when she has an idea for a book she's like the Ancient Mariner and stoppeth one in three. In this she's rare: the norm is for writers to guard their secrets as long as possible. Many of us refuse to give a clue about work in progress, never mind letting a soul glimpse a manuscript before it's finished. This isn't because we are super-confident and have no need of reassurance. Far from it. We are afraid that an unkind word, or at any rate one that falls short of fulsome praise, will so deter us that we can't bear to go on. And if anyone *should* oblige with fulsome praise, well, then we won't trust it and will wonder how he could be so blind when we are full of doubts and know the work to be flawed.

Besides, if you want a second opinion on your work, who *can* you show? Who will understand it as well as you do? Writers who attend writers' circles, where they are obliged to read their own work aloud for general criticism, presumably develop a resilience that leaves most of us in awe. Do they go on to finish those stories and novels or are they put off them? Say they absorb all the advice flung at them and let it influence their writing, can they feel that what emerges at the end is their own work?

The only person whose judgment about a partly finished piece of work is valuable is the writer. *You* know what your aims are and can decide for yourself whether you are achieving them. Another person will be bound to erect the goal posts in a different place, and you will be hurt when he says that you have missed them.

Once you have produced a second draft, which is to say a correct and tidied up version of your first draft, you might profitably seek an opinion. The ideal person to give it is a sympathetic friend who loves reading crime and suspense fiction. It matters that you are judged by someone who is familiar with the type of fiction you are trying to write. Other friends might be more literary, or have other qualifications which sound impressive, but unless they are sympathetic to the genre their response will be inadequate.

A knowledgeable fan will be competent to put a finger on weaknesses and mistakes. Keen readers of the genre know when a writer has fumbled the planting of the detective's clues or failed to squeeze the most from a tense situation. Listen to your friend's comments, the objections as well as the praise, and you can learn what the reaction of the average reader of the genre might be.

Working on your novel 7

Write on

Continue writing, following your Chapter Plan and keeping a Record of what actually goes down on the page. As the pile of paper beside you rises you will find the Record increasingly useful when you need to search for a particular incident or character.

Reading over

Make a habit of reading over your previous day's work before you begin the next stint. This is better than doing it at the end of a tiring session. A fresh mind is quicker to spot flaws and keener to correct them.

Characters

Once you are past the first chapter also pay attention to the way your characters develop.

- Are you asking anyone to act out of character?
- Have you dropped clues to the way your characters might react when the crisis comes?
- Are your minor characters kept in their places or hogging the action?

Reading list

Margaret Atwood, *Bodily Harm.*
Dick Francis, *Whip Hand.*
Lesley Grant-Adamson, *Dangerous Games.*
Graham Greene, *Brighton Rock.*
Andrew Taylor, *The Barred Window.*

8

FIRST DRAFT AND MOMENT OF TRUTH

We must grant the artist his subject, his idea, his donnée: our criticism is applied only to what he makes of it.   Henry James

The end of your first draft calls for a celebration. A restrained one, anyway. You have, at the very least, got your story down on paper in a series of scenes enriched with dialogue that develops the action and casts light on the speakers, and you have brought matters to a decent climax.

Depending on your temperament, you have in your possession a beautifully clean manuscript with hardly any crossing out and over writing, or a muddled sheaf of papers so elaborately annotated that only you can make head or tail of it. Whether you and your manuscript are at either of those extremes or somewhere in the middle, what you have reached is an important milestone on the road to a novel. You have not reached the end.

New writers are inclined to hope it's the same thing, and one can see the temptation when they are neat workers who have produced clean manuscripts. There's something rather authoritative about a cleanly typed or printed out document. One is more reluctant to challenge it than one would a handwritten text or one where the author's hesitations are recorded in scribbles and scrawls. It will probably, though, contain as many failings as the roughest looking first draft.

Turning the first draft into a second draft good enough to be shown to a publisher can be daunting, especially if this is your first time around the course. Things you were pleased with reveal themselves as banal or inadequate. Perhaps you realise a scene or a conversation was unintentionally copied from a book you had read, and then you feel a fool and a fraud. It can seem as though wherever you look you meet disappointment, that everything you tried has fallen below the standard you were aiming for. Well, if you are finding faults, you are on the right path. Reading over a first draft demands clear-sightedness and few illusions.

Actually, many experienced writers hate the prospect of reworking their texts, whether at this stage or later on when an editor points out errors or potential improvements. Treat the task as a challenge. Finding a solution to the shortcomings of a text challenges your ingenuity because you won't want to put in or take out passages that will throw other aspects of the novel out of kilter. There's a great satisfaction to be had from this kind of work well done, and it's an essential part of a novelist's job to do it.

— Editing —

Maybe it seems odd for me to be mentioning editors' recommendations already, when this chapter is devoted to looking over your first draft, but a thorough job done at an early stage can prevent a major overhaul later. For now, you have to be editor as well as author, and cast the coldest eye over your novel.

Try to be systematic about editing your work because you can get so involved in the story that things you ought to be considering go sliding past without your notice; and, in the same way, by concentrating on the small adjustments you may fail to focus on the overall picture. By floundering from one perspective to the other as you go along you will lose momentum and end up spending more time on it. Added to which you will do neither properly.

I suggest you begin by reading the whole book through and concentrating on the broad picture. The idea is that you pretend you are a reader and what you are concerned with is the general impression and the spinning out of the story. This reading should give you a sense of the pace and reveal whether the characters speak and act like credible people; whether a reader would care about the fate of the central character; whether existing scenes succeed in quickening the pulse; whether the ending is satisfying; and whether the theme is consistent throughout. In other words, you are attempting to judge the book as you would a novel written by anyone else.

Although you are playing at being a reader, you will be a reader that takes notes instead of merely grunting dissatisfaction at faults in the construction. Mark the pages where you notice flaws: the pace flags, the story meanders off course, there are contradictions, a dialogue misses the point or is too long, and some parts are plain boring.

Too long or too short?

No doubt you will spot fine examples of two popular blunders: writing episodes too briefly, and missing the opportunity to make scenes vivid, because you were concentrating on moving the story along at a lick; or writing too much about everything, instead of selecting the important events, and causing the pace to drag. As long as you have novels by fine writers on your shelves, reliable advice is to hand. Pause and read a chapter or two by an author who has used the tempo you are aiming at.

Where your writing is too tight, notice how scenes can be improved by adding detail or, say, pointing up the conflict between characters by using dialogue to give their arguments. Dialogue always makes a scene more alive. If your pace is sluggish, notice how experienced writers pass over unnecessary scenes in half a line. You may spot a published example similar to this:

> ❛ She went to the corner shop for cigarettes and was home five minutes before the bomb went off. ❜

Now, you didn't actually wish to read about the trot to the shop, the pleasantries with Mr Patel behind the counter, the fumble for loose change in her purse, the rain starting to fall as she came back in through the garden gate, did you? Me neither. In your text you may have written the equivalent of the scene with Mr Patel, and be justifying it because the woman is thinking something essential to the plot during her trip. But why not let her think it another time, rather than tuck it away in an otherwise irrelevant scene?

The way I have written the sentence retains the cigarette-buying trip, which I take to be either a detail about her character or a way of removing her from the house to meet the demands of the plot, but keeps up the pace. In fact, the contrast between the mundane activity in the first half of the sentence and the explosive second one is a useful weapon in the armoury of the crime and suspense fiction writer. It jolts the reader. And it increases the tempo.

In his own words

Dialogue which, correctly used, adds a lively dimension to a novel can be disastrous when it is not. Be critical about those conversations your characters are having. The commonest mistake is to let their exchanges go on too long, so that they chatter on about their domestic arrangements for three-quarters of a page after the relevant information has been conveyed to the reader. Make a note to cut and rearrange conversations that drift.

Occasionally, authors appear to back off and let a speaking character take control. The typical scene is one where John, say, is explaining a lot of background material to Seamus. No doubt it's essential for the two men to have this meeting and you presumably had a purpose in letting the information be delivered in John's own words. Maybe you indicate later in the book that John was deceiving Seamus by putting a gloss on the truth.

Whatever your motives, the effect on the reader will be disconcerting because the internal rules of your particular novel have been broken. Up to this scene, he will have been used to reading a narrative broken up by short sections of dialogue, or else to reading a story told largely in dialogue and with a small proportion of straight narrative. But suddenly here's a character delivering an uninterrupted speech covering several pages. It is a narration within the narration.

This type of scene is more likely to occur in thrillers and spy fiction, where an agent has to be briefed before dashing off to adventure, and you may argue that it's virtually a convention of those forms. But if you aren't writing one of those, or you prefer not to offer up the slab of text, you might like to ameliorate the effect of John's long speech.

First, trim it if you possibly can. Then break it into sections, so that you have turned it into a number of long paragraphs. In between these, you may slip brief paragraphs which indicate John's own private thoughts: his boredom with his subject; his doubt about Seamus's ability to grasp the details; his eyes straying to the clock on the wall because he has a lunch date; his foot resting on the open lower drawer of his desk; a recollection of the missing man who was the previous one he briefed on this subject; or the fly fussing around the plant on his desk. The details will enhance John as a character and may either emphasise what he's saying or provide a counterpoint.

And then there's Seamus. Assuming that you don't want him to speak and interrupt John's flow, you can devote short paragraphs to his mental reactions to what John is saying, his gestures, and his observations of John. Kept within check, the device of cutting away from John to his listener helps to keep the silent Seamus in the reader's mind, and cures the problem of the novel degenerating into a lecture.

───── Clarifying theme ─────

As we saw in Chapter Two, you don't need to choose a theme so much as identify it. As the story develops on the page, so the theme clarifies. Some practised authors are always well into a novel before they realise what it is, and it's not uncommon for it to dawn upon them while they are reading the first draft. By the time you finish reading yours you will almost certainly be sure what the theme is, although you might have despaired up to this point of ever discovering it. When the revelation comes as late as the read through, or when it comes during the course of writing, you will have more work to do. Lucky writers find their subconscious has taken care of the details, but they need to comb through the text, anyway, to ascertain that.

It's possible you will want to entirely rewrite some early scenes to make the theme more evident. You might be able to achieve the same effect by adding a scene. Equally, you might decide to cut a scene that is out of keeping with the theme. Tinkering with the imagery and other details might suffice. Before making any alterations at all to your first draft, you could have a special read through just to consider how and where to improve the theme.

On your initial reading of the first draft, your pencil may slash through sentences that reveal themselves as superfluous and underline phrases you suspect are repetitions. You might become doubtful about the relevance of whole scenes and feel the story gets bogged down. Maybe it occurs to you that a character could usefully make an earlier appearance, or at any rate be referred to before his current debut. Perhaps you spot a loose end, where something in the story hasn't been explained away. As the spy master was absent from his office on the crucial date, the reader will expect to be told the reason.

In places, a haziness might have crept into the writing because you are unclear about police procedure, or the physical effects of the murderous attack, or the forensic evidence the killer would have left at the scene of the crime, or the distance from the Underground station to the house, or the procedures for visiting a man in prison or an MP in the House of Commons. The signals for more research are unmistakable.

―――― **Improving: the big things** ――――

Keep your notes on your first reading brief so that they don't delay you. When you have reached the end, you should consider them carefully rather than rushing ahead with changes. The obvious method of correcting a flaw might produce a worse one.

Suppose you feel you ought to tighten (by which I mean trim to make crisper) a scene in chapter three. As it stands, chapter three is unwieldy: too many things are happening in too many settings and the effect is confusing and slows the pace. You have marked a section you would like to move. You can't drop it altogether because the information it contains is important to the development of the plot. The obvious place to put it is in chapter four, but doing so will interrupt the build-up to a thrilling episode. That won't do either. To insert it there would spoil the build-up, and for three reasons: the extra length, an additional character who doesn't appear in chapter four, and the different tempo.

Of these three objections, the last one is the least serious. You can swiftly rework a short section to match the pace of the chapter to which it's to be added. Just read through the chapter, to catch the rhythm of it, and begin rewriting. Deciding what to do about the other problems requires cautious consideration. Perhaps it crosses your mind to abandon the idea of slipping the section into chapter four and you skim through chapter five to find a slot for it. Ah, but by chapter five everyone in the story knows the information revealed in the troublesome section. Chapter five won't do either. Back to chapter four. How would it be if the extra character were dropped from the section, and the section were hacked back to a few lines? Hmm ...

By weighing up the pros and cons of each move, you can arrive at the best solutions for your novel. But, as you see, the quickest fixes may cause more damage than they cure. Thinking through the full effects of each potential change can save you a lot of reworking, both at this stage and later on when the book is in the hands of an editor.

If you are writing your Record in a book with facing pages, it's ideal to use the blank pages opposite each chapter to record your decisions about changes, and what you are trying to achieve. A typical note might read:

> 'Make it less obvious Serena was killed when she was shot. Adds mystery if detail is held over until Dermot mentions it in chapter eight.'

Or:

> 'Tension lags. Cut shopping scene and write new link between Dottie's hysteria and Det. Insp. Wizard's suspicion her robber was escaped killer.'

There may be a number of things that remain unresolved and read like this:

> 'MUST liven up scene on boat. Revenge theme needs to be more obvious.'

Extra research is best done before you move on but that's a counsel of perfection. Remember, though, that if you leave it until later the additional information plus corrections might mean that further changes in the text are inevitable. Learning that the type of gun fired leaves an exit wound larger than an entry wound, alters what the neighbour saw when he rushed through the door. Knowing that a killer would have had to strike repeatedly with the blunt weapon you handed him means that for each blow there was another chance of fibres from his clothes, his car or the rug in his flat being deposited on the body. Discovering that your hero can't knock on the prison door and ask to see a prisoner, but must await an invitation by Visiting Order through the post, can upset your timing.

Improving: the little things

When you have decided what needs changing and how to do most if not all of it, you are ready to go through chapter by chapter checking on the relatively small points. Pinpoint areas for improvement as you go.

Underline any phrases or words you fear you have used frequently; any wording that seems too fancy or inappropriate in other ways; anything that causes you to stumble instead of reading smoothly on. Read aloud because you may have made changes to a chapter since you previously did so. It's remarkable what a difference hearing the words spoken can make to your appreciation of them. My favourite example of a line which couldn't possibly have got into print had the author read it aloud is this, from an American crime novel:

6 You sonofabitch!' he yelled under his breath. 9

Try saying it, aloud.

Working on a word processor, you can easily run a check on words you suspect are being over used and then replace them with alternatives. Without benefit of modern technology you can keep a list of those you realise are becoming a problem and alter them when they crop up as you read on.

In this genre we run a special risk with our vocabulary because we are always dipping into the pool of words that convey tension, nervousness, excitement and fear. Check that you haven't used the same few to exhaustion. A thesaurus will supply you with alternatives, and so will reading well-written crime fiction. When swapping words for the sake of variety, be alert to the tension in the scene. You want it to increase, not fade. Therefore, when you have to change 'fear' twice, use the weaker alternative first. It's fine to have your hero experiencing trepidation on the first page of chapter six and terror as the scene reaches its climax seven pages later. But swap them around and you have nonsense.

By the way, do your characters have five senses or do they only see and hear? Smell is especially evocative and don't forget taste and touch. Because we 'picture' scenes in our minds and 'listen' to the dialogue, it's easy to concentrate on the visual and aural and underplay the rest. By the same token, have you revealed their emotions through gestures? A character may say a few calm words but give away an underlying emotion by clenching a fist as he does so.

Clichés are another hazard. When a character is scared the hairs stand up on his scalp, his spine tingles, his palms sweat... True, all true. That's the way human beings react. But we are dealing with fiction, not life, and if you can come up with fresh wording, all to the good. Beware, though, of being too fancy. An elaborate piece of imagery might only result in the reader objecting: 'Look, if his hair's standing on end, why don't you just say so?'

Using appropriate imagery – the dead flower heads in the killer's garden; the tangled water weeds that symbolise the victim's entrapment; the shadows of the Venetian blind that fall like prison bars across the bedroom of the man on the run – you enhance your story. Brief though they may be, strong visual images stick in the reader's mind.

But they aren't on the page because they are beautiful or poetic, although they may be more memorable when they are either of those. What makes them valuable is that they encapsulate something of the novel. In the crime and suspense genre they are most effective when they refer to death, fear or the other black things that are the stuff of our fiction. Given luck, such images arrive automatically while one is writing. Others are dreamed up when the first draft is being improved.

Pay attention to the words that start sentences and paragraphs. As I mentioned in Chapter Four, if you are writing in the first person, be vigilant that the word 'I' isn't scattered more liberally than absolutely necessary. When it starts a paragraph it makes its presence very obvious. And how have you coped with tenses? Active ones are a sure way of increasing immediacy and tempo.

Flip through your manuscript and look at the beginnings and endings of the chapters. Do you manage to capture interest at the start of each new chapter? You might like to begin occasionally with dialogue, to vary the look of the pages. And have you a hook at the end of each chapter, to coax the reader into the following one?

In other kinds of fiction authors are inclined to emphasise chapter endings, by recapitulating what a character has learned and adding a detail that, quite often, states something which has already been made obvious. (*'After that he went out of the door, leaving it on the catch as he usually did. The path was damp after the rain.'*) The effect is a natural break and a dying fall. Better not, especially in crime and suspense fiction. Whatever you contrive, the end of a chapter suggests a convenient time for a reader to put down a book and switch on the television, go to sleep or do whatever else is on offer. Fight him. Even in relatively quiet chapters you can entice him with a hint of intrigue. He won't realise how you are playing him, he will only know that he couldn't put the book down.

———————— **Book ends** ————————

Finally, here are some book ends. Your last words on the subject are almost as important as your opening paragraphs, because these are the lines that linger in the reader's mind when he closes the book. A good ending is one that provides a satisfying conclusion to the story, and also creates an appropriate mood.

Authors of detective series often conclude with a reassuring low key scene as their hero puts the unpleasantness of the case behind him and the reader is invited, by implication, to do the same.

In *Cabal*, a case for Aurelio Zen, Michael Dibdin chooses a dramatic alternative.

❦ ... Now the shock was over they were reassured to realize that the body plummeting to earth amid a debris of broken glass must be a spectacle of some kind got up to divert the shopper, an optical illusion, a fake. Clearly no one could have fallen through the enclosure overhead, as solid and heavy as vaulted masonry. It was all a trick. A moment before impact the plunging body would pull up short, restrained by hidden wires, while the accompanying shoal of jagged icicles tinkled prettily to pieces on the marble before melting harmlessly away.

In the event, though, it turned out to be real. ❦

Manuel Vazquez Montalban, the leading Spanish crime writer, sends his detective Pepe Carvalho on a reflective walk through Barcelona at the end of *An Olympic Death*. Montalban is one of those writers whose setting is paramount. Carvalho notwithstanding, the star of the novels is always Barcelona.

❦ ... And he followed the last sloping bit of the Ramblas down to the port to see if the encounter with the woman of his dreams was really going to happen. He sensed that this was the last time in his life that he was going to be able to behave like an adolescent, ignoring the reality of age as dictated by calendars and national identity cards, and he allowed his legs to carry him down to the docks, picking his way through the congested traffic and keeping a wary eye on the hysterical drivers, until he arrived at the water's edge. On the surface of the dirty water, in among the oil slicks and the garbage on the surface, he saw the body of Claire floating, with her geological, translucent eyes, and that smile which concealed as much truth as it conveyed. A smile that was like a mist of spray. He closed his eyes, and when he opened them again all he saw was the water, like a dirty mirror, and the bulky outlines of boats that were so firmly anchored that they looked as if they were set in rock. ❥

In his suspense novel, *The Music of Chance*, Paul Auster simultaneously finishes off the book and his hero.

❧ At the precise moment the car hit eighty-five, Murks leaned forward and snapped off the radio. The sudden silence came as a jolt to Nashe, and he automatically turned to the old man and told him to mind his own business. When he looked at the road again a moment later, he could already see the headlight looming up at him. It seemed to come out of nowhere, a cyclops star hurtling straight for his eyes, and in the sudden panic that engulfed him, his only thought was that this was the last thought he would ever have. There was no time to stop, no time to prevent what was going to happen, and so instead of slamming his foot on the brakes, he pressed down even harder on the gas. He could hear Murks and his son-in-law howling in the distance, but their voices were muffled, drowned out by the roar of blood in his head. And then the light was upon him, and Nashe shut his eyes, unable to look at it anymore. ❥

Margery Allingham, breaking the conventions of the traditional detective story in *The Tiger in the Smoke* while retaining Mr. Campion, ends with a quieter death than Auster's.

❧ Beyond the bay the sea was restless, scarred by long shadows and pitted with bright flecks where the last of the winter sun had caught it. But the pool was quiet and very still.

It looked dark. A man could creep in there and sleep soft and long.

It seemed to him that he had no decision to make and, now that he knew himself to be fallible, no one to question. Presently he let his feet slide gently forward. The body was never found.❥

The final page of Geoffrey Household's classic thriller *Rogue Male* is devoted to a written confession which is all the escaping hero carries into his new life. He ends with this.

❧ I begin to see where I went wrong the first time. It was a mistake to make use of my skill over the sort of country I understood. One should always hunt an animal in its natural habitat, and the natural habitat of man is – in these days – a town. Chimney-pots should be the cover, and the method, snap-shots at two hundred yards. My plans are far advanced. I shall not get away alive, but I shall not miss; and that is really all that matters to me any longer.**9**

——— Working on your novel 8 ———

Fault finding

Although I have outlined aspects to check once you have finished your first draft, it's also useful to look out for the same things while reading over each completed chapter as you go along. Once you identify failings you can make an effort to avoid them in succeeding chapters.

Scenes

- Are your scenes too long because you have padded them out?
- Are they too short because you have missed opportunities to develop interesting ideas?
- Have you used passive tenses for exciting scenes where active tenses would be better?

Dialogue

- Is each character consistent in the way he speaks or have you failed to differentiate the voices?
- Do the exchanges of dialogue go on too long?
- Is anyone lecturing instead of having a conversation?
- Have you enlivened scenes by letting your characters speak for themselves instead of having the narrator use reported speech?

Characters

- Do your characters have five senses?
- Do they convey their emotions by gesture?
- First person hero? Too many 'I's?

Chapters

Flip through your manuscript and look at the beginnings and endings of the chapters.

- Have you varied them?
- Do you manage to capture interest at the start of each new chapter? You might like to begin occasionally with dialogue, to vary the look of the pages.
- Have you a hook at the end of each chapter, to coax the reader forward?

Title

What are you going to call your novel? As you add each title to your list of possibilities, put an explanatory note beside it in case its relevance later escapes you. If you have a suspicion that the title has been used before, say that too.

Reading list

Margery Allingham, *The Tiger in the Smoke.*
Paul Auster, *The Music of Chance.*
Michael Dibdin, *Cabal.*
Geoffrey Household, *Rogue Male.*
Manuel Vazquez Montalban, *An Olympic Death.*

9

BEING PUBLISHED

*An amateur writer thinks if a publisher turns down a book there's
something wrong with the publisher. The professional thinks
there's something wrong with the book.*   Ed McBain

Getting published has never been easy but there are ways of improving your chances. For instance, it ought to be obvious that you should
submit your manuscript to people who publish the type of thing you
have written, but every day of the week publishers are inundated
with packages from hopefuls who haven't taken that into account at
all. By looking on the shelves in book shops, noticing who publishes
the books mentioned in crime reviews in newspapers and magazines,
and by consulting annual reference books, you will become familiar
with the names of publishers who have developed crime lists.

The manuscript

The manuscript you offer should appear professional and easy to
read. Type or print it out double-spaced on A4 paper, using one side
only. Allow wide margins, at least an inch and a half on the left for
the copy editor to make her marks. Leave space at the top and bottom
of the pages, too. Indent all paragraphs. Use paperclips, not staples,
to hold chapters together.

Should you number pages throughout the book or each chapter separately? Agents, I know, favour doing it consecutively. But it's imprac-
tical because a late change made in, say, chapter three will throw the
rest out of order and you then face reprinting the entire book.

Publishing houses use various methods of page numbering. As you don't know who is going to handle your manuscript, you will do best to number chapter by chapter. If each page is marked with the number of the chapter as well as the page – for example, Chapter 3, page 9 – you will avoid confusion.

Next, the title page. On this you put your name or pseudonym, your address, the title of your novel and an estimate of the number of words in it. If you are using a word processor it's a simple matter to instruct the machine to count the words in each chapter, so that you can add them up. But if you are working with a manual typewriter you will have to rely on the time-honoured method of calculating. You do it like this. Count the words in your first few lines, divide by the number of lines you counted, and you will arrive at an average number of words per line. Then count the number of lines on the page and multiply.

Instead of posting off the whole manuscript it's preferable to send the first two chapters. A stiff envelope will protect them, fancy binding is unnecessary. Enclose a letter asking whether the publisher would like to see the rest of the book. Mention the title, the approximate length, and say which category of fiction it comes into, such as thriller or detective story. Add a succinct résumé of the novel, just a paragraph. Before committing anything to the post remember: always keep copies of your manuscripts and letters.

Some publishers acknowledge receipt of manuscripts, so at least you know yours is lying in an office awaiting a verdict. In other cases the thing disappears into limbo until months later when you get an excited letter or telephone call saying they are interested in buying the book. Or until the postman drops it through your letterbox because they aren't.

Editors are optimists. They have to be. They are bombarded with manuscripts and approach each one in hope. I asked my editor to name three things guaranteed to put her off a crime or suspense novel. Not surprisingly, top of her list came illogicality. 'The faintest hint is fatal.' Second was being patronising. 'Writers let their middle-class prejudices show. They make policemen and shopkeepers illiterate because they think them lower class. It's a mistake to alienate readers. Potential readers include everyone, from dustmen to dukes.' Her third hate was authors striving for politically correct language. 'It's immediately outdated. Plain English is always best.'

Sorry

Letters of rejection are usually couched in friendly and encouraging terms, and may include advice about other publishers you could try or, indeed, which particular editors at other houses might be approached. Reasons might be given for the verdict having gone against you. These might relate to the novel's failings or the publisher's disinclination to take on any more crime writers. But, encouraging or not, you have been turned down. Unless the letter specifically invites you to do so, there's no future in discussing your work any further with that publisher.

Persevere, that's what you do next. You flick through the returned chapters to check for marks or other damage, reprint the title page plus the first and last pages because they will be tatty, and you start the process again. It used to be frowned upon for authors to submit books to more than one publisher at a time but, given the months long delays before publishers respond, it's becoming more common.

I'm deliberately not advising you to rework your novel in the light of remarks made in a letter of rejection. Novice writers are tempted to do so, feeling that after all those months of lonely toil here's a professional judgment and surely they ought to abide by it. Well, no. The letter is a polite 'No, thank you,' and although it may strike you as personal and applicable to your work, in reality it will be a standard letter.

No publisher is harsh enough to send out letters saying: 'My God, *The Burst Balloon* is the most awful thing we've read all year! What on earth possessed you to send it to *us*?' However much they hated it, the letter will be tactful. Supposing they felt the book or you as a writer had potential, they might helpfully draw your attention to weaknesses. A letter in this category is the one that beguiles you to rewrite. But, set it aside and await replies from other publishers, and you will discover how subjective these judgments are. One will say your novel was let down by poor characterisation while another will compliment you on memorable characters. One will remark on the thrilling ending while another will say it sagged. One will admire your pace and narrative drive while another will say it was slow and lacked suspense.

Naturally, when there's a consensus you would do well to follow the combined advice. And, having made the changes, you could write to the more encouraging editors and say so and ask whether they would like to see the improved version. Perhaps they won't, but the new draft will stand a better chance when you submit it elsewhere.

—— From manuscript to book ——

Once your manuscript is accepted it will lead a chrysalis existence before emerging transformed into a published book. You will catch glimpses of it from time to time: when it's edited and copy edited; when page proofs need to be read; when your advice is sought on the wording for the catalogue and blurb; and when you are shown the cover. The chrysalis state can last more than a year, depending when your publisher plans to bring out the book. Although books may be published every week, publishers' catalogues are issued twice a year. Before it can appear, your book must be described in the catalogue and enthused about by the salesmen who take orders from shops.

—— Editing ——

For you the most interesting, and perhaps the most challenging, part of the process is editing. Once a contract has been agreed your editor will arrange a meeting to discuss the text. If you live too far away to go and see her, queries and suggestions can be dealt with by post instead. Prepare yourself for the meeting by reading your novel as it might be several months since you have done so. Take along a note-book, and ask her whether she would like you to bring a copy of the manuscript, too.

This is the meeting at which the major decisions are taken. Should there be more about Bryony's background? Should that sequence relating Cartwright's previous adventure be trimmed? Would it be better for Sniffer the dog to winkle out the drug smuggler earlier in the plot? Are you sure the entrance to the Eiffel Tower is where you said it is? And so forth. But don't feel dispirited at the growing list of things to check and changes to make. Better to thrash out problems now than wait until the reviewers start grumbling about you waffling on about Cartwright, and not knowing your Eiffel Tower from your Tower of London.

Your editor may specialise in crime and suspense fiction, in which case she will have an exceptional understanding of the requirements of the genre. My novel *Threatening Eye* (see Chapter One) demonstrates the small but significant changes a novel may undergo to please a knowledgeable editor. By the end of the story B is shown to be the murderer and A escapes with his shady secrets more or less intact. In my final paragraph A's colleague visited the churchyard where dreadful things had happened, and reflected sadly 'as dead leaves rattled against the gravestones.' This was, I still feel, a poignant conclusion. But my editor's adjective was for it was 'lame', and she felt the book would be improved *as a suspense novel* if it ended with A's viewpoint. I went home and wrote a coda that warns the reader that the despicable fellow is still at large. And thus the novel ends with a frisson instead of a sigh.

Beginners sometimes have a fanciful idea of the amount of work an editor is prepared to do on a novel. Recently I read an autobiography by a writer who was angry that her first novel was published as she had written it. She assumed that it was the publisher's responsibility to reshape and polish. It's true that occasionally one hears of editors supervising the rewriting of a book by a novice, but this happens only in exceptional circumstances. Perhaps the central idea of the book is thought to be sufficiently original to warrant this; or the writer has inside information on a topical subject; or the writer is a celebrity whose name will ensure high sales. Whatever the reasons, they don't apply to you and me.

After your meeting, you will have to fly home and tackle the agreed corrections and changes. Soon is good, but thorough is better. Unless you have made alterations on almost every page, there is no need to print it all out again, just the altered pages. Beware, though. Changes to the text invariably demand changes to page numbers. This is what you do when the new material about Bryony's background overflows from page 11 and wrecks the numbering of the rest of the chapter. After page 11 you introduce a new page and number it 11a. At the foot of page 11 you add a note that '11a follows'. A long insertion might call for 11b and 11c, and so on, before the narrative continues on page 12.

Copy editing

Once your editor has approved the changes she will send your manuscript to a copy editor, (the American title line editor is also used) who will go through line by line and pick up all the small points. Poor spelling, variations in the spellings of characters' names, confusing sentences, muddles and blunders of all kinds will be pounced upon. Sometimes she will raise an objection to something that's perfectly all right as it stands but, rather than think her a fool, consider whether it isn't worth changing the offending lines, anyway. If she, a practised reader, has misunderstood, then the average reader might do so too.

Proof reading

One of your duties will be to read page proofs once your novel is set in type. This gives you a chance to spot missing lines, literals (errors in type-setting, usually misspellings), ugly word breaks (when words run from one line to the next), and details of that sort. With modern methods of computer setting, it's rare to be presented with a typographical mess and the task isn't onerous. It requires attention, that's all. A tip for keeping your eye on the job, and avoiding being caught up in the story, is to cover the text with a ruler or sheet of paper, sliding it slowly down the page as each line is carefully read.

An invitation to read the proofs is not an invitation to rewrite your novel. Indeed, publishers discourage authors from doing so by warning that, beyond a certain limit, the cost of the corrections made at their request will be passed on to them. Your editor will explain the house rules regarding proofs, including what colour pen you should use to mark the pages. A few publishers present new authors with style books which include the standard proof readers' marks. I have included a list of them at the end of this chapter.

Titles

Picking the perfect title is a distinct talent. Some authors are fortunate enough to have brains crammed with apposite quotations, or to have the knack of adapting a piece of contemporary slang or jargon. Although you may be aware that the ideal one has escaped you, don't submit your novel without a title. That creates the impression the story has you stumped. An untitled manuscript is an unfinished piece of work.

Also, pity the poor staff at the publishing house faced with discussing 'that one about the man who comes home and finds his wife's run off with the VAT inspector while all the time she's dead in the potting shed.' Be kind, give them a handle. *Something Nasty* or *The VAT Man Cometh*; or anything.

Titles are regularly committee decisions reached by author, agent and editor. Even if you are happy with yours someone may offer a better idea. I remember being a bit disappointed when Faber regarded *Patterns in the Dust* as too soft for a sharp detective story but I agreed to change it to *Widow's Walk*. When it was discovered that another book called *Widow's Walk* was coming out, the committee was floored and we reverted to the original.

I don't propose that it's one of the great titles but it does fit a story about recurring situations, a secretly buried body, and the significant clue of footprints in a supposedly unused room. Also, it turned out to be a title that people remember. I'm frequently asked which poem the phrase comes from. Well, as far as I know it isn't a quotation except from the novel itself.

Original titles are rarer than one might hope. Publishers try to avoid those that have been frequently used but, when you are dealing with a genre, obvious ideas tend to be repeated. Bacon gave crime writers a gift when, in his essay on revenge, he called it 'wild justice'. We too, too eagerly accept it. Robert Browning considerately supplied 'the dangerous edge of things'. We use *The Dangerous Edge* with alacrity. *The Book of the Dead* and *The Dying of the Light* are two more that seem to circulate forever in the catalogues.

Wiser to avoid the popular lines, perhaps, but how can you sidestep them? There are two speedy ways of ascertaining whether you have picked a hackneyed title. Feed the name into the computer at your local public library and see how many entries pop up on the screen; and ask book shop staff to run a similar check with their computerised *Books in Print* directory.

Covers

Authors with bright ideas about covers are always heeded. After all, the writer has thought longer and harder about the book than anyone else and may have a suitable cover in mind. Once you know who your publisher is to be, see whether you can think of something that fits in with the house style. For instance, some publishers put the title and author's name in a panel in a certain position on the cover, while others use big writing over, perhaps, half the space. Both designs impose limitations on the way illustrations can be used.

Although authors often grumble about the results, publishers put much effort into designing covers, either in house or using design agencies. It's very important to them to create one that has impact when seen from a distance in a shop, as well as close up. Colours and style of lettering come into the equation as well as choice of picture.

Your contract will probably state that you are to approve the cover, and this usually means that you are initially sent a rough sketch and later on a finished design. You don't have a veto but you may have spotted a flaw no one else has, so speak up.

Blurbs

Blurbs tend to be another committee job. It's not the least unusual for editors to claim they can't write and send you a rough version for you to titivate. By the blurb I mean the few lines on the inside front flap of your hardback loose cover, or the back cover of your paperback, that tell the reader about the novel and its author.

In crime and suspense fiction, there's a risk of giving away too much in the blurb. The aim ought to be to entice the reader by letting him know what kind of intrigue or adventure is on offer, and to encourage him to believe he will be in the hands of a competent writer. Unfortunately, blurbs become résumés of the story and instead of hooking the reader they let him escape, feeling he knows what it's all about. Don't do that. Tantalise.

This example of the résumé blurb comes from Kingsley Amis's *The Riverside Murders.*

> ❻ The hero of Mr Amis's flesh-with-blood novel is a fourteen year old boy hovering hopefully on the brink between experience and initiation. The delicious and totally mind-consuming prospect of sex, which tempted him into orgiastic games with his friend Reg, is now centred on the less satisfying (at present) but equally hot pursuit of those mysterious, formidable creatures – girls.
>
> Riverside Villas is the scene of Peter's exploits – and someone's crime. The victim, dripping wet and with a bleeding head-wound,

staggers in through the french windows of No. 19 and dies. Motive – none that the police can pinpoint. Weapon – a weird spiked club, no trace of fingerprints. Opportunity – only one suspect has a foolproof alibi.

As the mystery deepens, further attacks and an enigmatic note reveal the presence in the small country town of a learned, thoughtful criminal. Only Peter guesses the truth, a dangerous truth that leads him to the river bank by moonlight ... ❯

And so on.

By contrast, this is the blurb that coaxes you to read Margaret Atwood's *Bodily Harm*.

❮ Rennie Wilford is a young journalist on a seemingly innocent assignment to the Caribbean island of St Antoine. With growing horror she is caught up in a lethal web of corruption, espionage and violence. In this small world nobody is what they seem: from the suspicious Dr Minnow (he tells her blood is news) to the burntout Yankee Paul (does he smuggle dope or hustle for the CIA?) who offers her what seems to be a no-hooks, no-strings affair ... ❯

This one, from William McIlvanney's *Laidlaw* is equally concise.

❮ The torn and murdered body of young Jennifer Lawson is found in a Glasgow park. Laidlaw, assisted by Detective Constable Harkness, is given free rein in his search for the murderer. He is not, however, alone in the hunt; two other forces, neither of them legal, are after the man. And as Laidlaw threads his way through the city and its inhabitants, the race develops: against time and against death. ❯

Agents

Is it a good idea to have a literary agent? Yes, agents are guardian angels. They are listed in the same directories as publishers, and a number have considerable experience of the crime and suspense fiction market. Your initial approach should be a letter describing your novel and asking whether they would like to see it. Although agents stipulate in the directories '*preliminary letters essential*', beginners persist in submitting manuscripts and some make the mistake of enclosing their rejection letters. There are agents who fight shy of finding publishers for authors of first novels, because it can be a time-consuming affair. If you succeed in hooking a publisher yourself, you could invite an agent to negotiate the contract for you.

But let's suppose an agent takes you on to her list. Her rôle will be to look after your interests. There are two aspects to this. One is to advise you about developing your career. And the other is to win the best possible financial deals from your publisher as each book is offered, and to sell any rights in them that the publisher doesn't buy.

A typical contract might stipulate that the publisher pays you an advance on royalties of £3,000 for the right to publish in hardback and paperback in certain English language countries, half to be paid on signature of the contract and the rest on publication of the hardback. Once the publisher has recouped his £3,000, you will be said to have 'earned off' the advance. After that further royalties will be paid to you, perhaps ten per cent on hardbacks and seven and a half per cent on paperbacks, as sales continue.

It's a curious thing that, although topicality is often cited as one of the attractions of crime and suspense fiction, these titles can maintain small but steady sales over many years. Your agent will strive to get you a good share of any money the publisher might make by 'selling on' rights, for instance to another company who wants to produce your book in big print for the visually impaired; or to serialise it in a magazine; or to read it on the radio. Usually, she will retain the American rights (for the English language countries that form part of the American market), foreign rights, television and film rights, and talking book rights, in the hope of selling those separately.

—— Minimum terms agreement ——

If you can't interest an agent in handling your prospective contract, the next best thing is to ask the publisher for a Minimum Terms Agreement contract. The MTA is the standard that a growing number of publishers are adopting after negotiations with the Writer's Guild and the Society of Authors. MTAs differ from publisher to publisher. Be cautious, though. Publishers who are signatories don't unfailingly offer those conditions to authors who don't request them. Copies of the MTA are available from the Guild (sae to 430 Edgware Road, London W2 1EH) and the Society (sae to 84 Drayton Gardens, London SW10 9SB).

On the screen

Film and television rights are the two that everyone asks authors about. 'Is it going to be a film? Is it going to be on television?' On bad days you may feel that, as a mere writer, you don't have a legitimate existence if you have to say no. Film and television adaptations are a welcome bonus. They can make you more money than your original contract and all the subsidiary sales put together. Funnily enough, so can having your hopes repeatedly dashed.

These rights are usually handled by a different agent from your literary agent. She may have a colleague who specialises in the field, or she may have an arrangement with a specialist agency. When your book is sent to likely film makers and television production companies, one of them may buy an option on it. This means you have granted them the option to buy film or television rights within a certain period of time. Payment for an option may be as low as a few hundred pounds or may run into the thousands. The period may range from six months to several years. Under the terms of the contract the company will probably have the right to renew for one or two further periods, paying you again each time. Should it decide to take up the option, a fatter sum will be paid for the right to make the film or programme.

Usually, though, the company loses interest when the option runs out and the agent sells another option to another company. An author with a series character can do very nicely when a film maker chooses to buy an option on the hero, in the hope of adapting all the stories about him. As you see, you can earn considerable sums from film and television companies without a script being written or an actor stepping in front of a camera.

Writers whose work is adapted are frequently disappointed by the results, and those who succeed in being effectively involved in productions are rare. Still, that won't stop you being thoroughly excited on the day your agent telephones to say you have sold an option or, far better, the rights. Enjoy it. Dream a little. As one writer who has been around the course many times remarked:

❛ You can't ever be sure your book will be on television until you switch on your set and see it. And even then you mightn't recognise it. ❜

Foreign rights

Sales of foreign rights, to publishers in other countries who want to translate your novel for their markets, can also make up a significant part of your income. Your literary agent will also have a colleague who specialises in foreign sales. Contracts and conditions vary. Some countries have their own traditions of writing crime fiction (France, Italy and Scandinavia) but others (Germany and Japan) have long been importers. Since the collapse of Communism there's been a boom in crime fiction in Eastern Europe, especially in Russia. The Moscow bestseller lists now feature home-grown writers alongside Dick Francis and John Grisham.

The Russian example proves a point about crime fiction in general. Because it's largely topical and reflects the society about which the author is writing, it varies from country to country. What the Russians have to say, and the manner in which they say it, is inevitably unlike the work of writers in any other countries except for those in the former USSR.

A country's social and political history always influences its fiction. The stable government and settled existence that Britain has enjoyed for centuries provides the rationale for British stories. Countries that have a turbulent history produce crime novels which echo that volatility and violence. A Mexican writer encountering the modern version of the English classic detective story would be puzzled by the restraint on the part of the author and characters, while we might be equally sceptical about the behaviour and attitudes he described.

Working on your novel 9

Continue to write, following your Chapter Plan and keeping your Record.

Characters again

Everything in the novel depends on character. Your cast must do your bidding and you must not ask them to do anything that doesn't suit their nature as you have described it. Keep an eye on them.

- Are your characters under control or are they proliferating and threatening to cause confusion?
- Should you be amalgamating some or cutting someone out?

Titles

- Does your title catch the tone of your novel?
- Is your title easy to say? You will want people to ask for it.
- Imagine it on the cover. Is it so long that it couldn't appear in big type?
- If it begins with 'The' or 'A' consider whether it would look more elegant without the article.

Proof-readers' marks

Familiarise yourself with the marks you will be expected to use when you correct page proofs.

Changes are made on the text and the marks are made in the margin on the left or on the right of the pages.

Your editor may refer to the pages of your manuscript as folios.

Margin	Instruction		Text mark
a λ	insert		λ
Y	insert:	space	rainy⅄day
, λ		comma	pigs⅄ cats⅄ dogs
⊙λ		full stop	said⅄ Then
⊙λ		colon	these⅄ ices, sweets
; λ		semi colon	all⅄ but
⅄ ⅄		quotation marks	λNo,λ he said
᧒	delete		ⱥ r̶a̶n̶d̶
᧒	delete:	character	pigⱥs
᧒		word	she was w̶a̶s̶ out
⌒	close space		she w⌒as out
⊗	wrong font		⟨she⟩ was out
⊘	reinstate deletion		she w̶a̶s̶ out
‡	lower case		ⱼeans

≣	upper case	jeans
=	small caps	ladies
⊔⊔	italics	ladies
⌇	roman	(ladies)
⌐	run on	cats, pigs, dogs
⎍⎍	transpose	pigs, cats
⊏	take over	in the end. Dis- aster
⊐	take back	to the very end.
⌐⌐	new par	end. Next
⊏	indent	Next

Reading list

Kingsley Amis, *The Riverside Murders.*
Margaret Atwood, *Bodily Harm.*
James Buchan, *Heart's Journey in Winter.*
John Grisham, *The Firm.*
William McIlvanney, *Laidlaw.*
The Writers' and Artists' Yearbook.
The Writer's Handbook.

10

THE VOCATION OF UNHAPPINESS

Writing is not a profession but a vocation of unhappiness.
Georges Simenon

Occasionally the creation of a novel goes so smoothly that the writer says it appears to be writing itself. Without his conscious thought, the characters go about their business, the story swings along from chapter to chapter, the pace is ideal, every day's writing produces bright ideas just when they are needed. The dream novel. It isn't impossible that your first novel is one of these and when you read through the first draft, you struggle to find faults. Well, if this is happening to you, you are enjoying a very special piece of beginner's luck. The only snag is that it leaves you unprepared for your next book to be less of an inspirational flight and more of a calculated achievement.

Long ago, when I was a journalist, a colleague asked me whether I would like to write a novel and I said, 'No.' While he was murmuring surprise I explained that one alone would be no use, because what I wished for was the talent to write a number. 'Otherwise,' I said, 'I wouldn't feel I was a real novelist.' Do you feel the same way that I did, or is the novel you are working on to be your single venture into fiction, because you have one pressing idea which you feel compelled to write about?

If you go on to make a career of writing novels, you will discover that working on each succeeding book will be different. Some require lots of research, some throw up numerous difficulties and some skim along. Whatever your experience with your first novel it's unlikely it will be repeated exactly with your others. Of course, as you produce more and more you will accrue skills and experience to help you over the hurdles, and you will develop an individual approach and a rhythm to your work. But the special pleasure of writing the first one can't be equalled.

The joy of completing and selling a first novel is considerable. Family and friends celebrate with you. Your editor is thrilled that she has added to her list a potentially money-making new talent. Her career and yours have become entwined, and you can rely on her to be very positive about your future. Yet she may also be voicing the occasional word of caution which, in the general excitement, you may overlook.

The second novel

What she would like to tell you, but without spoiling your moment of glory, is that writing a second novel can be particularly difficult. In fact, there's a prize for them (the Encore Award presented by the Society of Authors) which acknowledges the peculiar challenge the second one presents. Too many of them fall short of the standard of the first, and editors are forced to reject them or to insist on major rewriting. When either of these things happens it's a devastating blow to a writer's confidence.

There's no magic formula for avoiding the pitfalls of a second novel, but here are some ideas based on the experiences of several writers. The first came to me as a piece of advice from an agent who had seen plenty of authors stumble over second efforts: write the second one before the first is published. Usually there's a gap of a year between selling a book and seeing it in the shops. Let that be your space in which to tackle the second novel. Doing it this way means that however much your life and privacy are disrupted when number one reaches the bookshelves and the reviewers, you aren't going to be put off your stroke. You already have a good follow-up novel in the pipeline at the publishers, and you are safe.

The second is this. Unless you are committed to writing a series of similar books featuring the same characters, which you almost certainly will be if your first offering is a detective story, you might consider writing a different kind of book the second time. Suspense instead of detection, for instance. You avoid the risk of repeating your first book too closely, and you keep your writing fresh and broaden your skills. When I began writing I believed that the best writers within the genre were those capable of suspense as well as detection, and so I set out to do both myself. I think it is still true now.

What's gone wrong?

But supposing everything goes wrong. When your second novel seems a disaster, perhaps because you can't finish it or the editor hates it, you must cling to the belief that the problem isn't that the talent that produced your first success has vanished but that you aren't using it fully. This can happen for a number of reasons including over confidence and being deserted by the beginner's luck that saw you through the first book. Perhaps, though, your life has changed between books. This might mean you have given up the office job or your charity work to concentrate on writing, and you are missing the stimulation of working with people around you. Or you might have moved house, assuming that a quiet country location would increase your production as a writer, but you miss your friends and haven't settled down.

Oddly, the success of the first novel might be hampering you. There may have been a shift in the way you perceive yourself, and the way others perceive you, but the influence of a first novel often takes a more obvious form. If your publisher has done a reasonably good job of promoting you and getting your book reviewed, you might be disturbed by being thrust into public view.

In the public eye

The publisher's publicity department will be gratified if you have been interviewed by local or national publications, and chatted on radio or television. Perhaps you have been doing your duty at literary festivals, appearing on stage with more experienced writers and being expected to produce opinions and make sensible contributions to discussions about the genre. As readings in book shops or at literary events are popular now, your publisher might have initiated you into those.

Poets do very well at readings because it's easy to give a flavour of their work. Writers of mainstream fiction are able to select a scene which demonstrates the quality of their writing. But the poor crime writer, whose novels are very tightly structured, has to plunder the text for a few paragraphs that can, more or less, stand alone. Too often he seizes upon one of the lighter scenes, which may be well written but hardly gives a taste of the book that was reviewed as 'haunting', 'a chiller' and so forth.

When it comes to readings, writers who let ideas drip, drip, drip through the novel are at a disadvantage compared to those who occasionally slow the action to allow Detective Inspector Wizard to ponder at length the ways in which the proposed bypass will ruin for ever the pleasant pastures around Snoozytown, and how the town is symbolic of all those ancient English towns being threatened with modernity, and so on and on and on. Writers are loathe to read aloud their first pages, although I can offer no explanation for this. My view is that it makes sense to do so, providing the scene introduces a principle character, sets the tone and pace of the story, and indicates the mystery to be explored.

Unless you are fortunate enough to enjoy a little harmless showing off now and then, these sudden ventures into public life might fill you with trepidation. Most writers admit to feeling self-conscious and embarrassed but with practice the reluctance wears off. Even when they love it all, the disruption these outings cause to a novelist's work is out of all proportion to the amount of time actually spent on them. However, they are part and parcel of the modern writer's job, and we have to be thankful for them rather than fret about being dragged away from the desk halfway through writing the last chapter. How much better, though, if the second novel has been delivered to the publisher before such distractions arise.

Reviews

Reviews are another hazard. Even favourable ones come as mixed blessings because they drag the mind away from work in progress. Bad ones, of course, can spoil your day. Because of this, many writers claim not to read them. Generally what they mean is that they don't read reviews when they appear although curiosity forces them to glance through them eventually.

Like most things in life, book reviews are subject to fashion. From time to time, crime fiction enjoys a vogue among books page editors and the space accorded to reviews increases. Then it falls out of favour and the space shrinks. At the time I am writing this, newspapers are short of paper and what they can buy is exceptionally expensive. The result is that the number of books pages has been reduced and crime reviews have become less frequent than we have been used to in the preceding ten years.

Newspapers like to do what they call round-ups of crime fiction, which means that the books page editor selects a batch of novels, from the dozens sent in by publishers, and asks a reviewer to devote, perhaps, five hundred words to a handful of books. The result is that although a reviewer may be dazzled by your novel he isn't allowed much space to say so. But on the same page another reviewer might be floundering in an attempt to find any merit at all in a mainstream novel by an unknown writer whose book has been allotted eight hundred words accompanied by a portrait photograph. It's rare for a writer of crime and suspense fiction to be treated with the same seriousness. No, this isn't fair to writers and neither does it provide a decent service to newspaper readers. The only consolation is that writers in other genres, such as romantic fiction, fare worse than we do and are seldom reviewed at all.

By tradition reviews are published when hardback novels appear. Their importance is twofold. They give the publisher a clue how many copies of a paperback edition he might sell, and favourable ones provide a compliment that can be reprinted on the cover of the paperback. Therefore, the reason too many crime and suspense novels are touted as haunting, chilling and what have you, is that those are the phrases that spring to the reviewers' minds. Given the strictures of conveying in a few words what a novel is like, you can understand why they opt for the tried and tested. Even so, it's amusing when a reviewer who deals in clichés squanders his precious words on objecting to an author using them.

Since some publishing houses began to skip hardback publication and issue novels in paperback straight away, the attitude to reviewing paperbacks has changed. Books page editors are no longer able to argue that, as they only review new work, paperbacks don't count. These days your novel may be included in a round-up of hardbacks and later in a round-up of paperbacks.

Bad reviews

Lest what I say next sounds like pique, I must preface it by stressing that I have been lucky with reviews and have every reason to be grateful to the critics. However, such luck isn't universally shared and even the most admiring reviews may contain an unwelcome caveat. When we talk about bad reviews we inevitably mean ones with which we don't agree. This may be because the reviewer has disliked the novel or has been disappointed in it, but his reasons may remain mysterious because he has no space in which to justify them.

Quite often it seems that he has gulped a batch of novels and become sated. It's hardly your fault if he jibs at 'yet another story about a private security company losing the Crown Jewels.' How were you to know other writers were using the same subject? And, anyway, the coincidence has hardly altered a word of your novel, has it? Yet he has wasted newsprint to accuse you of lack of originality.

Reviewers have extraordinary power to distress, and they don't always fulfil their obligation to consider a book for what it is. Before you waste a morning wringing your hands over a review, ask yourself why it was written like that. Often reviewers are fellow crime writers, and it's a perfectly respectable way to supplement one's income; but if, for instance, they are pledged to approve all hardboiled detectives and detest the crime novel that's so close to mainstream you need Sherlock Holmes's spyglass to see the gap, then they have no right to let that prejudice influence their comments on your work. We aren't free to choose which kind of fiction we are capable of writing; we can only hope what we do is good of its type. A conscientious reviewer will know this.

Faced with a hurtful review by someone whose tastes you don't know, check what he says about the other novels in the round-up. As it's virtually impossible to comment on a handful of novels by accomplished writers without praise and congratulations creeping in, their absence in an entire column is telling. Occasionally, a reviewer will strain every sinew to avoid giving a flattering cover line for paperbacks. Over the years I have detected two sorts of reviewer playing this game. One is the type who believes his own novels to be underrated, and the other resents younger and fresher authors entering his field. Their behaviour is ungenerous but you will survive it.

The rôle of the reviewer is altogether strange. He's paid to point out your triumphs and disasters, but when he charges you with inventing implausible characters or letting the pace flag in the middle, he doesn't have to go to the trouble of saying how it might have been done better. After initial annoyance, the wise novelist pauses to wonder whether the fellow might possibly have a point. Should more than one reviewer voice the same reservation, the answer is bound to be yes. Or *almost* bound to be ...

When *A Life of Adventure* was published several reviewers added a quibble that it was my weakest detective novel. I was mystified because it involves no detection whatsoever. Then I realised that on the front cover was a quote referring to me as the novelist who had *'brought the detective story into the nineties'*. The publisher's slip in applying this to a different sort of book had coloured their reading.

Reviewers pay most attention to newcomers and leading writers in the genre. They have a duty to tell readers what is new, and to say whether the big names are on top form. Unless you understand the system it can be depressing when, a year or two after your debut, your tally of reviews drops because you have lost your novelty value but haven't been selected to join the happy band of those who may not be ignored.

A final word about reviewers. Their tenure is short. That used not to be the case and if, say, the man from *The Guardian* took against your hero or your use of the semi-colon, you faced displeasing him year after year. Equally, the perceptive woman who heralded you as the natural successor to Edgar Allan Poe would echo her accolades. Now, though, they come and quickly go. On mornings when you are burdened with unflattering reviews, it's a comforting thought.

No, on second thoughts let's give the final word to Dr Johnson.

❛ He that writes may be considered as a kind of general challenger, whom every one has the right to attack; since he quits the common rank of life, steps forward beyond the lists, and offers his merit to the public judgment. To commence author is to claim praise, and no man can justly aspire to honour, but at the hazard of disgrace. ❜

More, please

There are writers who relish entering the same fictional world in book after book. Aficionados of the detective story, readers and writers alike, get enormous pleasure from slipping into a familiar setting with characters they recognise. Thriller heroes regularly feature in several adventures, and lovers of spy fiction would have been sadly cheated had John le Carré retired Smiley after one novel. Let's suppose that when your first novel is accepted your publisher asks you to write a series about your heroine, Jane Fisher. Let's also suppose Jane is a detective who lives in a provincial city in England. She's likeable, and you have made her sufficiently interesting for your publisher to believe that readers will want more and more of her.

If you originally had no inclination to write a series, you might be unsure how to cope. A series is a different proposition from writing a one-off novel. For instance, you have to take a longer view about the fate of characters. As a writer you will appreciate that to kill Jane's lover would give you a shocking scene. It would push her near to breakdown, spur her on in her search for the truth, and be more satisfying artistically than having him merely grazed. But, as a series writer, you will have to bear in mind that if he's killed, Jane herself will be altered permanently; and you will have to replace him in later books, either by another lover or by having a colleague or someone else grow close to her and fill the vacant rôle of confidante.

Readers have phenomenal memories and should an author accidentally change details about a character's setting or life, they pounce. In the friendliest way, of course. To save yourself embarrassment, you will need to keep a record. A card index file is the traditional way but these days recording details on a word processor is favoured. As well as setting down information about a character, it's worth mentioning where, in previous books, full descriptions appeared. Then you can look them up when you wish.

Also, there are topographical and geographical facts to remember. A map is a necessity, whether it's of a real setting you are using or a place you have made up. A floor plan of your houses and other buildings will prevent you slipping up by mentioning in one book that Jed Sly, your hardboiled detective, clattered downstairs from his office and in another that a passing child pulled faces at him through his office window.

A writer told me recently that she had abandoned a series because she felt hemmed in. Her publisher had wanted her to stick to a medical background and keep the same hero and setting. She believes she could have coped with any two of the elements but being asked to use all three over and over again was too restrictive. I think she made a good point. We become writers because we wish to use our imagination and many of us find it stifled when we are hedged about by rules. We would rather do without them, even though obedience to a publisher's dictate would ensure a book a year and the subsequent steady income. These are matters of temperament, and you might discover only by experience whether you are happiest with the safety net of a series or the dangerous freedom of life without one.

Trilogies and quartets

There's another type of series which ought to be mentioned here, one that seldom occurs in crime and suspense fiction. I mean the trilogy or quartet in which an author writes linked stories developing a theme. While they can be read as individual novels, they also hang together as one entity. Writing them isn't the same as writing an ordinary series because the author's intention is different. Instead of simply shaping a story into a novel, you also have to create a progression. Each novel must grow out of its predecessor.

My Rain Morgan and Jim Rush novels illustrate the differences in constructing the two types of series. The gossip columnist Rain Morgan arrived fresh at each murder case and I told a story about loyalty, revenge or whatever was apt. Although she developed as a character from book to book and facets of her life altered, there was nothing to prevent me carrying on with that series for ever, had I wished to. By contrast, when I decided to write about the American conman Jim Rush I planned a set number of books to chart his moral decline. There is a symmetry in the series. At the beginning of *A Life of Adventure* he's caught but by the end he's breaking free, thus inverting the traditions of the thriller; in the sequel, *Dangerous Games*, he has gained an uneasy freedom and at the end he's escaping again; as the third novel opens he's free, but by the end is caught in a predicament from which there is no way out.

So you see, although Jim's calamitous adventures can be read as separate stories they are in fact stages of the same one. The real story isn't about him infiltrating the Chelsea set in the first book, or searching for sunken treasure in the second one, or pulling off a scam on the Costa del Sol in the third. No, the overall story is about an alienated young man striving through greed and through guile to recreate his world, but losing everything. For this kind of series theme is paramount.

———————— **In reference** ————————

As your work progresses you will acquire, perhaps willy-nilly, your own reference library. Like all writers you should own a good modern dictionary, an encyclopaedia, and one or two books about the use of modern English; but you will also need on your shelves books on subjects such as police work, psychology, true crime and forensic science. Fortunately, these are readily available in cheap paperback editions, and earlier books may be found in your public library or in secondhand book shops.

With the surge of interest in true crime during recent years, the experts have been unstintingly helpful to the aspiring crime writer. Several eminent pathologists and retired police officers have published accounts of investigations that were highlights of their careers, and written them for the layman. These books contain invaluable guidance about methods of dispatching victims and, ultimately, of getting caught. Beware of relying on out of date information, though. Forensic science has adopted DNA testing, for instance, in the years since some of these experts were at work and your present day fictional detective must be up to the mark.

However, modern scientific advances make no difference to the fact that it takes less time to drown in fresh water than at sea (four minutes compared with between eight and twenty); or that the skin of people who die of carbon monoxide poisoning is pink; or that the coroner may release for burial a body in a murder case, after evidence of identification has been given at the opening of an inquest, but the body may not be cremated lest exhumation is later required. Whatever the circumstances of your fictitious crime, the information you give the reader about the case must be factual. Habitual readers of crime fiction may well be more knowledgeable than you, and they are quick to spot faults and flaws. Never under-estimate your reader.

——————— **The sociable crime writer** ———————

Once your first novel is published you will be elegible to join the unusually sociable world of the crime writer. We are envied by the lonesome writers of mainstream fiction who may have no opportunity of socialising with other writers. You, though, will qualify for the *Crime Writers'*

Association; the *Detection Club*; *AIEP*, the international association of crime writers; the *Mystery Writers of America*; and you will be welcome at conferences on crime writing at home and abroad.

The first meeting of the *Crime Writers' Association* was convened by John Creasey in London on November 5, 1953. His twin purposes were to raise the standing of crime fiction and to provide an opportunity for writers to meet socially. Monthly meetings (at a club in central London) and quarterly lunches (in several regions of the country) include talks by experts such as the police, customs officers, pathologists, or social workers involved in topical issues. The association also publishes anthologies of short stories. Members are kept up to date by a monthly newsletter, *Red Herrings*.

During the autumn there's a weekend conference, and in May and December the annual awards are announced. The *Diamond Dagger*, sponsored by Cartier, is presented in May for a body of excellent work, and has been bestowed on authors including Eric Ambler, Ruth Rendell and P.D. James. The recipient is chosen by the *CWA*, which isn't the case with all the awards presented in the association's name at the December awards dinner. Winners of *Gold* and *Silver Daggers* for the best crime novels of the year, the *John Creasey Dagger* for a first full-length fiction, and several other awards for fiction and non fiction, are selected by a panel of critics. There is also an annual short story competition.

When you are ready to join, write to the secretary with proof that you are a published author. Vanity publishing, which means you have met part or all of the cost, doesn't count.

The Detection Club dates from 1930. Following hard on the heels of Father Knox, it required its members to swear their detectives would detect crimes properly without recourse to 'Divine Revelation, Feminine Intuition, Mumbo-Jumbo, Jiggery-Pokery, Coincidence or the Act of God.' Nowadays it's a dining club and its members are as likely to write thrillers or suspense fiction as detective stories, so the conventions have fallen into abeyance. One rule persists: you don't apply to become a member, you wait to be invited.

Once your book is published in the United States, the *Mystery Writers of America*, founded in 1945, is open to you. The range of awards it presents annually for fiction and non fiction are known as Edgars, after Edgar Allan Poe. Its magazine is the *Third Degree*. Women writers also qualify to join two other US clubs: *Malice Domestic* and *Sisters in Crime*.

One especially ardent American fan, the late Anthony Boucher, who was a critic with a fine grasp of the nuances of crime fiction in a changing world, is remembered in the annual crimefest called the *Bouchercon*. This conference usually takes place in the USA but has twice been held in Britain. Famous crime writers from around the world meet their fans at the *Bouchercon*, but they also meet new publishers, agents and talent-spotting television producers. After a weekend of giving talks, signing books and networking, authors attend an awards dinner during which prizes called Anthonys are handed out.

Nottingham has established itself as a centre of 'criminal' activities in Britain. Its *Shots in the Dark* festival, held each September, began as a celebration of crime films (*The Silence of the Lambs* had its first UK showing there) but included a couple of literary events. In subsequent years a full programme of literary events was added. The city's literary festival also includes crime fiction, and in 1995 the *Bouchercon* chose Nottingham as the venue for its second conference in England.

───── Working on your novel 10 ─────

Language

Your novel will be developing its own internal rules governing the use of language. They probably came to you naturally, but you must be consistent throughout the book.

In this book, for instance, I have used relatively few contractions of words. Another of my choices was to refer to the reader as 'he', rather than resort to the clumsy 'he or she'. But as a high proportion of women are employed in publishing, I assumed your editor and your agent would be women.

1 What have you decided to do about contractions? *It is* or *it's*? *Could not* or *couldn't*? You might feel that those two contractions help the prose slip by smoothly, but how do you feel about *he'd've* instead of *he would have* or *I mightn't've* in place of *I might not have*?

Some writers restrict their use of contractions to dialogue and are altogether sparing with it. Others use contractions in the flow of the narrative and, in a bid for realistic dialogue, use it liberally when characters speak.

2 A number of words have equally acceptable alternative spellings. (Judgement or judgment.) Use which you prefer and stick to it. Beware relying for guidance on the spelling check programmes on computer software. There's no substitute for an English dictionary.

3 Are you using appropriate imagery? An image that recurs, perhaps discreetly, during a novel is an asset.

Keeping up the good work

By now you have gone a considerable distance towards achieving your novel. Maybe you have streaked ahead with the actual writing, chapter upon chapter piling up on your desk. Maybe you have been slower about writing but are now confident about the way ahead and poised to get down to it in earnest. Whether you are on the fast track or not, you have put in a lot of effort. If you followed the suggestions for practical work, you will have a few scenes and chapters to prove that you are an embryo crime writer. Well done. You are on your way.

My next piece of advice is as important as anything else I've said. Please don't lose your momentum when you come to the end of this book. The enthusiasm you feel for the project in the early days *can* be maintained, just as long as you keep writing. There's always a danger, after writing courses of all kinds, that one rests on one's laurels, sets the work aside for a while, and then discovers one has lost interest. To reawaken interest in any kind of creative work that has gone stale is extremely hard, especially for the beginner. Your assets at this stage are your commitment and your determination to persevere. Don't let them fade away.

Reading list

Archbold, *Criminal Evidence, Pleading and Practice.*
Paul Benjamin, *New York Trilogy.*
J.H.H. Gaute and Robin Odell, *Murder Whatdunit.*
Dr Lindsay Neustatter, *The Mind of the Murderer.*
Keith Simpson, *Forty Years of Murder.*
Bernard Taylor and Stephen Knight, *Perfect Murder.*

Specialist bookshop

Crime In Store (and *Post Mortem Books* catalogue) 14 Bedford Street, London WC2 9HE.
Murder One, 71 Charing Cross Road, London WC2H 0AA.

11

SHORT STORIES

A short story is a way of indicating the complexity of life in a few pages, producing the surprise and effect of a profound knowledge in a short time. Bernard Malamud

A short story is not a brief novel. A novel can be used to relate the events of a lengthy period of time, can introduce the reader to an array of characters and take him into a range of settings. The novelist is allowed upwards of 60,000 words in which to achieve his effects: establishing and resolving conflicts, showing how characters evolve in response to the drama, enriching the tale with humour and despair, and always speeding towards an exciting climax. The short story writer is likely to be restricted to 2,000 words, or perhaps 5,000 depending where his work is to appear.

It ought to be obvious from the comparative brevity that the short story demands a different kind of storytelling; and yet, when beginners recite the outline of a short story they plan to write, it frequently turns out that what they intend to do is encapsulate a novel. This is especially true of writers who fancy they have an idea for a crime short story, and it's partly because there are technical reasons that make tales of detection difficult to bring off. More about this presently.

Although you may be setting out to become a novelist, you can't ignore the short story form entirely because published novelists are regularly approached by magazines and editors of anthologies who assume they have short stories to hand. Stories that appear in magazines and books, or on the radio, are useful publicity for you as a writer and they provide some additional income. A single story may, over the years, be sold to a magazine, broadcast on the radio and anthologised several times. Length of stories in magazines and books is a matter of fashion, so you will need to check current requirements when you come to write; but on radio the norm is 2,000 words because they are dropped into fifteen minute broadcasting slots.

What, then, separates the novel from the short story? The fundamental difference is that the short story focuses on an event. It might be the day that a pattern is broken: the burglar's wife shops him. Or perhaps it's about a dramatic moment: the bank raid. This is how V.S. Pritchett, one of the most admired writers of the English short story this century, defined the form in his introduction to *The Oxford Book of Short Stories* in 1981:

> ❦ A short story is always a disclosure, frequently an evocation... frequently a celebration of a character at bursting point. ❧

That is as true of the genre story as it is of the literary one.

As ever, the best advice to the novice writer is to study the work of the finest authors in the field. Of course you may go off and enjoy the masters and mistresses of a bygone age, but as a potential writer it's crucial that you read the best of the modern bunch because it's their work that provides the benchmark against which yours will be judged when it lands on an editor's desk.

Familiar names recur: Rendell, Highsmith and Dahl. Ruth Rendell is a prolific writer of crime and suspense short stories notable for their delicious irony. Patricia Highsmith is equally well known for her short tales of suspense as for her novels. Roald Dahl is another in their league. His *Lamb to the Slaughter*, in which the policeman helps eat up the murder weapon, a leg of lamb, is a classic, one of those brilliant ideas that leaves you wondering why no one thought of it before. But there are many other leading novelists in the genre who also write occasional stories, and by browsing through modern anthologies you will discover the numerous ways in which these yarns may be spun.

Viewpoint

Short stories are most commonly told from one viewpoint. Like novels, they are usually written in the first person (I) or the third (he, she, they), and few writers trouble with the second person (you). (Peter Carey did, in *Room No. 5*.) They usually have a linear plot, which is to say they start at the beginning of the episode with the burglar's wife having a change of heart, they describe what happened next (she takes steps to return the stolen goods to the owner), and then they say how it all ended (her husband was arrested on another matter entirely; or the owners were disgruntled because they had already made a fraudulent insurance claim far in excess of the value of the stolen property; or, while she was out of the house attempting to do good, the woman's own home was burgled).

The single viewpoint is often supplemented with brief glimpses of the action from the viewpoint of another character. Sometimes the second, or even a third, viewpoint is extensively used. If there's to be more than one viewpoint in your story, the shift between them must be adroit. The reader won't appreciate being swivelled about like a spectator at the ringside, but neither will he feel comfortable if you harp on one character for so long that he suspects you have forgotten the other. Each one ought to be kept gently in play.

You can use ploys to achieve this: as omniscient narrator you, the author, can refer to the absent one, perhaps by comparing the similar fears or habits of the pair or contrasting their attitudes. Another way is for the character who is present to refer to the other one, directly or indirectly.

Much of the effort that goes into creating a short story may be spent on trying out ways of telling the tale, rewriting until you are happy that the conflict and the characters' reactions to it, the workings of their minds and the tremors of their hearts, are revealed as entertainingly as you can manage. When or whether to change viewpoint may figure prominently in your deliberations.

——————— Catching the reader ———————

When a story is very simple, it's success depends totally on whether the writer is skilful enough to engage the reader's sympathy in the characters and their fate. You hook him by showing people in an interesting predicament. As you describe their efforts to resolve the problem, you tantalise with hints that encourage him to read on. Finally, you conjure a satisfying ending, which may mean a twist in the story or a revelation but may be merely the hero's acknowledgement of changed circumstances.

Exactly as in the novel, the ending should feel 'right'. Please surprise the reader into thinking: 'Well, I didn't guess that would be it'; but please don't astound him so that he mutters: 'Oh, no, that's quite impossible.' Lay your story out with care – the clues or pointers to the conclusion all fairly in place, although not emblazoning the truth – and he will be delighted that you have nicely entertained him rather than cheated him.

Depending on the subject matter, your story may be violent or reassuring, but it should always be vivid because you have to make an immediate impact. There's little time and space to acquaint the reader with your actors and their turmoil. You don't have the luxury of gradually building characters, settings and all the other elements as you do in a novel. This means that the better you know your characters before you begin writing, the more easily the story will come.

Developing an idea

Writing a short story can take you as long as writing a novel. In terms of craft, stories are closer to the poem than the novel because they are distillations of ideas and, in literary short stories, the language may be highly wrought until it has the precision and intensity of a poem. Even using the plainer language of the crime or suspense story, you may have to produce many drafts, during which you rewrite scenes to bring them alive, develop ideas that were previously only touched on, reject some things and invent others, and tighten and polish the language.

Luckily, most writers occasionally have a story that emerges fully formed so I mustn't give the impression that it's always a slog. One of my most popular ones, *Members of the Jury*, was dashed off after the editor of a literary magazine telephoned begging me for one. Rather than be left out of his crime fiction issue I agreed, and then had to concoct 2,000 words to put into the post that evening. The resulting story has subsequently been read on Radio 4, appeared in an anthology and a women's magazine, and was used by a school's examination board.

The underlying truth is that all I did was delve into my memory for a real experience and give it a crime fiction spin. I had always vaguely thought that the situation could be turned into fiction and suddenly my chance had come to put it to the test. The reality was this. A coroner in a Midlands town developed the curious habit of inviting the same set of elderly folk to serve whenever an inquest required a jury. From the press bench I observed this pantomime for years, and was amused by the jury's comic self-importance and predictable responses. One woman demanded of police witnesses every single time: 'Was there any sign of a struggle?' For my fiction I posed *my* favourite question 'What if..?', and came up with a story told, chiefly, from her point of view. It's another afternoon of inquests, she's part of that comfortable little club, the jury; but this time she's also a murderer. And she has to ask the fateful question, because she always does.

No doubt you share my experience of noticing things that you believe would make a story, but having no idea when or how or whether to use them. A commission from an editor is the ideal way of being galvanised into action but, had I not kept a scribbled list of possible subjects in my diary, I mightn't have remembered the provincial jury when the call came. I was away from home, and without those jottings it would have been easier to say no.

The moral is when ideas for short stories occur to you, write them down. Maybe you have seen a fascinating person or an intriguing incident, or you have heard a phrase that starts your literary juices flowing. Don't lose them because these moments are the seeds of the short story. But wait. This is beginning to sound familiar. Didn't we say that this is how novels begin? Might these moments prove not to be short stories at all but incidents in a novel? How are you to know? Before you commit yourself to all the work entailed, you will want to be convinced that you sense the stirrings of a short story rather than a novel.

Short story or novel?

Judging whether your glimmer of an idea is suitable for a short story or a novel is tricky. Experienced writers might feel they know intuitively whether the idea offers them enough scope for development into a long fiction, or whether it's best kept to a short sharp form, but that's no help when you are a novice and daren't rely on your wavering judgment. Oh, for a mental litmus test that would produce results of pink for a novel and blue for a short story. Lacking one, try confronting a few questions. The first, and your actual idea has no bearing on this, is: 'What do you actually *wish* to write?'. Supposing you have been keen for some time to try your hand at a short story, it's possible that your subconscious has been working along those lines.

Next, write a paragraph summing up the story. Are you brimming with ideas that extend the tale? Perhaps you realise the protagonist has led an adventurous life before the episode covered by your paragraph, and that what you describe in the paragraph is a culmination of his experiences. Or perhaps his future opens up before you, a future that begins where the paragraph ends. Perhaps this character's story isn't the heart of the matter, after all. His actions, as you have written them down, may be the catalyst for drama in other lives, and those other lives are now revealed to you.

Providing that at least some of the ideas that rush into your mind are sensible ones, the indications are that you could have the bones of a novel. This doesn't mean that you should therefore write a novel instead. No, you remain free to concentrate on the incident that originally appealed to you and to make of that a short story. But, if your mind does *not* teem with fresh ideas that tempt you to believe you have the ingredients of a novel, it's certain you don't. And in that case, there's nothing to be gained by struggling to elaborate your idea because you will only spoil a decent short story.

Maybe you remain doubtful. You have a few additional ideas although not a flood of them, and you can't decide whether they are worthwhile. Very well, let's weigh up your central character. Is she strong enough to sustain a whole novel? If she's irritatingly scatter-brained, for example, it may be that 2,000 words is all you or any reader could tolerate of her.

—— Pitfalls of the detective story ——

And now for the special pitfalls of the crime story, and detection in particular. When you read crime stories you will notice that few of them are brief versions of detective novels, and that even those that feature an author's regular detective may show him in different circumstances. He may be on holiday, or out of his usual milieu for other reasons. This is probably not purely because the writer had a bright idea while he was himself on holiday, but because he's playing the numbers game.

The short story demands a small cast: three is usually claimed to be the ideal. But a *detective* story involves sleuth and possible partner, victim and killer, and a selection of suspects. I once had to itemise these for a magazine editor who was urging me to cut the cast list, of an 8,000 word story, to three characters because she believed her readers could not cope with another four.

Tackling the detective story, you will inevitably home in on the investigation at a late stage because the story needs to be focused on the solution to the mystery. This approach results in one of two situations: either the previous stages of the investigation have to be rapidly described, perhaps by the detective musing alone or discussing it with his colleague; or else the case under investigation is a rather slight and simple mystery. If the latter, it won't bear much resemblance to the full length tales of detection that flow from the same writer's pen. However, when a magazine editor commissions a story about a certain sleuth, she's primarily interested in seeing his name in her pages.

A popular way around the problem of reducing the detective form to suit the short story, is to let two detectives talk it over. Common devices are for a novice detective, puzzled about the case, to be asking Detective Inspector Wizard what put him on to the killer; or for the reader to be allowed to eavesdrop as Wizard tells his wife what he has been up to at work that day; or for Wizard to make his report (verbal, of course) to his superior officer. Writers of detective fiction love a challenge and they are clever with this format.

Successful detectives

While reviewers on literary pages are alert to new novels, collections of short stories generally pass them unseen. Ask, though, in your local library whose stories are popular and you will be rewarded with names that might otherwise have escaped you. Doubtless someone will mention Catherine Aird, the first recipient of the Golden Handcuffs award presented by Hertfordshire libraries to those who have made a significant contribution to crime fiction. Although writers cringe at comparisons, and especially when they are being measured against authors of an earlier age, there is some justification for critics who say she's as clever as Margery Allingham.

Injury Time is Catherine Aird's collection of short stories about Inspector Sloan, the hero of her detective novels. With sly humour, she writes tales that achieve the feat of feeling close to the traditional detective story in form while reflecting modern life. Just as in the novels, Sloan's short cases hinge on poisoning, legal niceties and medical knowledge. The clues are ingenious, in the finest tradition of crime fiction.

Steady As She Goes, the first story in *Injury Time,* has the elements of classic crime. A murder is committed in a house, in full view of a witness. The story opens with a short scene during which Inspector Sloan, accompanied by his constable, is briefed by his superior about an unusual death from antimony poisoning. Then there's a break on the page, a white space, and the story is picked up later when Sloan and his colleague interview the witness. Miss McCormack describes how her sister died after drinking a cocktail poured by her brother-in-law. The nub of the mystery is contained in her lines:

> ❢ And I don't know either how Paul killed Anna but I can tell you one thing. He did it before my eyes and I can't for the life of me think how. ❡

Neither can Sloan until he has heard about the finicking to create a striped cocktail. The final scene, the dénouement, takes place in the police car in a layby, with Sloan explaining to the constable the importance of specific gravity and his reasons for proceeding to arrest the dead woman's husband. The story is as neat a piece of deduction as any devotee of the detective story could hope for. Aird tells it in three conversations: between Sloan, his constable and his superior; between Sloan, his constable and the witness; and between Sloan and his constable. During those conversations we learn about two more characters: the dead woman and the murderer.

To write this type of story a writer requires fluency with dialogue. *Steady As She Goes* opens with a line of speech and finishes with one, and there are hardly any paragraphs in between that aren't enlivened with the voices of characters. Sloan's final remark, that it was *'a matter of knowing where the rainbow ends'*, suggests a title, but Aird wisely resisted mentioning rainbow in her title. It would have focused the reader's attention too closely on the cocktail's stripes and diminished the intrigue.

Once you have freed yourself of the constraints of detection, you may write your story in any way you wish and there's no one to gainsay you. In a short fiction you may risk an experiment that might seem foolhardy in a long one. Aspiring spy fiction writers may turn to Somerset Maugham's *Ashendon* short stories for proof of this. Critics claim their influence on the direction of the spy novel was as profound as Francis Iles's effect on the crime novel.

Finding a buyer

You have written your story but now what do you do with it? The publications you usually read don't carry fiction, or at any rate not the type of story you have produced, so where can you offer it? Magazines change their attitudes to fiction with every breeze that blows. For me to offer advice about outlets, let alone to suggest lengths you might aim at, would be hopeless. Annual directories for writers keep up to date and are to be found in the reference section of your local library.

It's safest to consult a directory rather than send your story to a magazine purely because you have noticed it publishes stories. Many magazines have a policy of refusing 'unsolicited manuscripts' and the stories you read in their pages will have been commissioned. When a publication stipulates a length for short stories, it's a requirement to be taken seriously because it probably equals one of their pages or a page and a half. There's always, I suppose, the faint possibility that an editor will be so entranced by your prose that she will ask you to cut an offering that's over long. But there's a probability that she will select instead someone else's story that's the correct size.

As a short story *is* short, there's no harm in submitting a copy of the whole thing to a magazine. Print it out double spaced on A4 paper. Number the pages. On each page put your name at the top on the left and a key word from the title at the top on the right. In the centre of a separate sheet of paper print the title and your name, and below that state the number of words and your address. The title page should look like this, with all the information immediately available (see over).

Attach a brief covering letter inviting the editor to consider the story for publication. Normally, you needn't describe the story, or yourself or the state of the weather. The only exception should be if you have a story set at Easter, for instance, and want to draw attention to its potential for an issue around that date. In these days of speedy reprints from word processors, you may like to add that you don't want the manuscript returned should it prove unsuitable. Surprisingly, magazines frequently ignore such requests and go to the bother and expense, anyway. Well organised ones will send you a note acknowledging receipt of a story that they don't reject outright. Final judgment may be deferred for months but there's nothing you can do about that except live in hope.

Death of a Novice
by
Andrea Duncan

2,000 words

Ms A Duncan,
20 Clifford Street
Harpenden
Herts.
Telephone: 123456789

Once in a while literary magazines fancy publishing crime or suspense stories. They pay a fraction of the rate you will earn from big circulation women's magazines yet it can be worthwhile selling to them. First, and excellent for morale, is the kudos of having a story in a literary magazine at all. And then there's the chance that it will be noticed by another editor or a radio producer, which was what happened to one of my stories in the relatively obscure *New Welsh Review*.

In hard covers

New writers who aim to begin their literary careers by publishing collections of stories are destined to disappointment. Publishers insist that they don't sell, and it's no use arguing that Ian McEwan and a few other literary figures made their débuts with volumes of stories. Unless there's a shift in fashion, you can't hope to become the Ian McEwan of the crime and suspense genre.

What about anthologies, then? How can you wriggle into those? It's chicken and egg. Once you are known as a writer in the genre you may be invited to contribute to an anthology. And once your work is in one anthology, you will be asked to submit stories to others. Publishers' budgets for anthologies are slender, so this is no way to make a living.

On the air

Radio, and in particular the BBC, can make your reputation as a writer of short stories. The BBC publishes guidelines for authors who wish to do any sort of writing for broadcast. Buy the booklet and keep up to date. But what are the general requirements for a story that's to be read aloud? Listen to the current output on Radio Four and you will be aware of the wide range of material that's bought. The only requirement is that the stories are good of their type. Competition is keen and standards high, especially as favourites from famous writers of the past turn up on these programmes, too. Having a story accepted is an accolade. Not much cash, I'm afraid, but plenty of cachet.

Working on a short story

1 You have an idea for a suspense or crime story. Write it down very briefly with the events in chronological order. Take the same decisions that you did for the novel:

- Who are your characters and what are their relationships? Remember to keep the numbers to a handful.
- Whose perspective, or viewpoint, are you going to take? Don't let the narrator report on events he couldn't have seen or quote characters whose conversation he couldn't have heard.
- Will you use the first or third person? Whichever you choose, don't forget to enliven scenes with dialogue.
- Which is the most interesting point at which to begin telling the story? You have to catch the reader quickly.
- How are you going to shape the story? Two popular ways are to start with a hint of the conflict or mystery, and build steadily towards a climax; or to start with a dramatic moment and finish with another, perhaps as truth is revealed or revenge is exacted.

- What sort of tempo and tone suits the story and the narrator? An elderly man reminiscing will have a more leisurely delivery than an anxious young man who expects to be arrested.
- Choose a length for your story. 2,000 words is popular.

2 You have an idea for a detective story. As well as answering the questions above, you will need to consider this when choosing a starting point:

- Are you going to start towards the end of the investigation and recapitulate all that has gone before? Or are you going to make it a simple investigation and follow it through?

Reading list

Collections

Catherine Aird, *Injury Time.*
G.K. Chesterton, *The Innocence of Father Brown.*
Roald Dahl, *Tales of the Unexpected.*
Patricia Highsmith, *Eleven.*
Somerset Maugham, *Ashendon.*
Ruth Rendell, *Collected Short Stories.*

Anthologies

1st Culprit, Chatto and Windus Annual of Crime Stories.
Crime Yellow, Gollancz New Crimes.

GLOSSARY OF LITERARY TERMS

allusion passing reference to a thing or person. To have your hero, sweltering on a hot day, grumble about the *unruly sun* would be to make an allusion to Donne's poem *The Sun Rising*.

cadence the rhythm of language, the rise and fall of speech; it is cadence, as much as vowel sounds, that differentiates accents.

characters people in a story.

contents *what* is said in a novel.

conventions common features of novels within a genre.

dénouement final clarification of a plot.

empathy being absorbed by a character.

first person narrative a character speaks directly to the reader; *I* did this and that.

figurative language fancy rather than straightforward descriptions, employing similes and metaphors.

form the *way* things are said in a novel.

genre a type of fiction.

hero central character in a novel; not necessarily a *good* character.

hypotactic sentences clauses are linked together by such conjunctions as *when, how* and *which*.

imagery see figurative language, simile and metaphor.

irony the meaning is contrary to the words; this creates a dry humour.

metaphor saying one thing *is* another; *he had a razor wit*.

motif image or incident that illustrates an aspect of the novel.

narrative the tale that is told.

narrator the person who tells the story; an *omniscient* narrator has an overview and reports everything; an *unreliable* narrator is one whose judgment of events the reader learns to mistrust.

paratactic sentences clauses are linked together by *and* and *but*.

pathetic fallacy attributing human feelings and actions to the inanimate; *the clock said it was ten to three.*

picaresque episodic adventures; the first picaresque story was *Don Quixote*; elements of the picaresque that occur in crime fiction include a quest marked by the appearance of a sequence of remarkable characters.

protagonist see hero.

reflexive the writer reminds the reader he's reading a novel; authors writing about private detectives seem prone to do this.

rhythm the way the prose flows.

simile saying one thing is *like* another; *his wit was as sharp as a razor.*

sub plot activities of a subordinate set of characters; or secondary story in which hero also features.

sympathy feeling for a character and his emotions.

syntax how meaning is affected by word order in sentences.

theme concept or idea which the novel illustrates.

villain the character whose bad actions disrupt the others' lives.

SOURCES OF QUOTATIONS

Books from which quotes are included in *Teach Yourself Writing Crime and Suspense Fiction*.

Chapter Two:

Raymond Chandler, *The Lady in the Lake*, Hamish Hamilton
Dorothy B. Hughes, *In a Lonely Place,* No Exit Press, 1990.
  (Permissions from Laurence Pollinger Ltd)

Chapter Three:

Ronald Knox, *Decalogue*, from *Best Detective Stories of 1928-29*
Francis Iles, *Malice Aforethought*, Dent. (Permissions from The
  Society of Authors.)

Chapter Four:

E.M. Forster, *Aspects of the Novel*, Cambridge lectures 1927.
Julian Symons, *Bloody Murder*, Pan

Chapter Five:

Georges Simenon, *The Hatter's Ghosts*, Penguin
Margaret Millar, *The Soft Talkers,* Penguin
Patricia Highsmith, *The Talented Mr Ripley*, Penguin
Len Deighton, *Berlin Game*, Hutchinson
Sue Grafton, *C is for Corpse*, Macmillan
P.D. James, *Unnatural Causes,* Faber and Faber
Ruth Rendell, *A Judgement in Stone*, Hutchinson
Walter Mosley, *Red Death*, Serpent's Tail

Chapter Seven:

Andrew Taylor, *The Barred Window*, Sinclair-Stevenson
Lesley Grant-Adamson, *Dangerous Games,* Hodder

Chapter Eight:

Michael Dibdin, *Cabal*, Faber and Faber
Manuel Vazquez Montalban, *An Olympic Death*, Serpent's Tail
Paul Auster, *The Music of Chance*, Faber and Faber
Geoffrey Household, *Rogue Male*, Penguin

Chapter Nine:

Kingsley Amis, blurb for *The Riverside Murders*, Cape
Margaret Atwood, blurb for *Bodily Harm*, Virago
William McIlvanney, blurb for *Laidlaw*, Hodder

Chapter Eleven:

The Oxford Book of Short Stories, 1981, Preface V. S. Pritchett, OUP
Catherine Aird, *Steady As She Goes,* from *Injury Time*, Macmillan

INDEX